The Fixtures and Fittings of
PERIOD HOUSES
1714–1939

The Fixtures and Fittings of
PERIOD HOUSES
1714–1939

Janet Collings

THE CROWOOD PRESS

First published in 2011 by
The Crowood Press Ltd
Ramsbury, Marlborough
Wiltshire SN8 2HR

www.crowood.com

British Library Cataloguing-in-Publication Data
A catalogue record for this book is available from the British Library.

ISBN 978 1 84797 237 8

Designed and typeset by Focus Publishing, Sevenoaks, Kent

Printed and bound in Singapore by Craft Print International Ltd

Contents

Introduction

This book aims to give the owner of an older house an understanding of the materials and features that have been used to create the house, and how these elements should be respected and cared for, rather than being stripped out of a house, to be lost forever.

Houses that retain more of their original character and have less modern intrusions are better able to remain 'timeless'.

Houses have evolved over the years and many parts of them have been added to or have had parts removed from them. Whatever has happened to a house is all a part of its history, and a history we, who are custodians for a relatively short period in the history of the house, must respect. We should only add elements to a house and avoid removing anything from a house, as it is all a part of our heritage. In addition, retaining all parts of a house and its fabric is very sustainable. Where changes have been made in the past, because there were no waste skips to take away unwanted rubbish, fixtures and fittings were re-used in other parts of the house. For example, if open shelves were being moved from a kitchen, then they might be put up in cupboards or other rooms, so that they were not wasted. In addition, this means that someone analysing the history of a house, is able to see what has happened to the house over the years. An historian is able to identify recent as well as older changes to a house, so whatever has happened to a house in its immediate past is all a part of its history; consequently care should be taken not to try to remove or obliterate this part of the historical record.

The types of alterations that have been carried out in the past are, to a certain extent, connected with the availability of materials to carry out the works. Prior to the railway network connecting up distant parts of the county, few building materials were used very far from the place where they were made. Also, at times when there was a scarcity of building materials and resources, such as during and after the end of the Second World War, when alterations were less likely to be carried out, due to the scarcity of building materials and labour for what would have been considered non-essential works – a lot of repairs were required for existing houses and then new houses needed to be built.

Where original or historical features have already been removed from a house, there are several options to consider. First, does anything actually need to be put back? The reason for this question is that replacing anything that has been removed from a house will involve using up additional natural resources and energy to re-create the lost feature. Perhaps the most honest approach would be to leave the house as found, and accept that the removal of certain features was a part of its history. There is also a fine dividing line between respecting the house for the type of house it is and not trying to add features to it to make it rather grander that it actually requires. For example, wishing to add ornate or decorative cornices to bedrooms, where in the

The overall appearance of a house relies upon all of its components.

The setting is important in helping to create the overall feel of a house.

Houses often relate to their surroundings not only visually but by having been built using the stone, timber and soil that surrounds them.

By being built from local materials, old houses were able to harmonize with the landscape, and by being designed with centuries of local experience, they were better able to cope with local environmental conditions.

particular type of house, there were either no cornices originally or they were very plain and simple.

The most important part of looking after an older house is to ensure that it is carefully and appropriately repaired and maintained. The difficulty is trying to decide what an appropriate amount of repair is and when such a repair may stray into the area of wasteful replacement. There is a subtle dividing line between these two concepts, but the best rule of thumb is to retain as much as possible of the existing fabric and only replace what is absolutely necessary; perhaps because it is completely rotten and there are no other ways of saving the building materials. For example, where the corner of a timber window has rotted, this area can easily be repaired by using metal brackets if the joints are loose or by splicing in pieces of new timber to replace the rotten ends of the existing pieces of timber. There are a number of advantages of this approach. The existing timber that was used to make the original window frames was perhaps of a more long-lasting and durable type of timber than is available today. In addition, it was probably seasoned more slowly by comparison with modern timber. Seasoning is where the timber, once it has been cut down, is laid out in a drying shed to dry out, naturally and slowly, which changes the size of the wood itself; ideally, this can take up to a year. The reason for doing this is that when the timber has reached dimensional stability and is cut into shape, it does not then expand and contract as much as it would if it were unseasoned or 'green'. The modern-day equivalent of natural seasoning is to use kilns to dry the timber in a much shorter space of time. In addition, the quality of the timber used is perhaps not of the same dense and slow-grown quality that was available up to the earlier parts of the last century, so any new timber is perhaps likely to be less durable than older and traditionally seasoned timber.

Total replacement, rather than carefully repairing using matching materials and splicing techniques, also means

that more of the original fabric is lost and, therefore, the history of the house is reduced for future generations to appreciate. This is why repairs are always preferable to replacements. But the need to even consider repairs or replacements might only be necessary where ongoing maintenance has been lacking. This means that, for example, windows and doors should be regularly painted, to ensure that the existing paint finish is continuous, so that water is unable to get into the timber and rot it.

Before looking at individual features of houses, the area of the country within which the house is located will give some clues as to the materials that were easily available and were, therefore, commonly used. The

Here the local tradition was for thatch and clay, plain tiles, both requiring a steeply pitched roof, but when this cottage was built, it could take advantage of slate imported over hundreds of miles and this meant that a cheaper, shallower roof could be used – this added another style to the locality.

naturally occurring materials under the surface of the soil, such as stone and clay, could influence the materials that were used to construct houses. Then there were materials like thatch that was a by-product of grain production and could be used to weatherproof roofs. Where there were specific industries, such as iron foundries, in the locality, these provided elements for houses, such as railings, door and window fittings, and rainwater pipes. The geographical location of a house could also influence the types of building materials that were used on the house. If the house was near to a river or, later on, near to a canal or to the local railway station, then this meant that heavy or factory-made building materials could be more easily transported over greater distances, which again could have an effect on what could be used on a new house. For example, Welsh roofing slates were only really used outside their immediate locality, once the railway network had been built.

How this Book is Organized

This book uses examples from the wide the range of materials and details that are found on houses in the United Kingdom, so that owners are able to identify, enjoy and appreciate the beauty and craftsmanship that they have inherited with their house.

The book is divided into three parts, with the exterior elements covered in the first part of the book and this is followed by a look at interior features in the second part of the book, with a final section about sustainability.

Building Styles

The style of house depended on the prevailing fashions, and when these fashions changed houses were often altered to reflect the change in taste. Nowadays, finding houses that have not been altered is rare and, as a result, very few houses survive in their original form or design. Medieval buildings were often made of timber framing in areas where there was timber, but with the Georgian period, a desire for change and solidity encouraged the use of bricks, so many older buildings were refaced using bricks to update their appearance to match the current trends. When the Victorian period allowed for the expansion of towns and cities through industrialization and better freight transport, this meant that new building materials were available to be used on houses that had previously been confined to using local materials. The Victorians were keen to show off their skills and, for example, developed bay windows as a contrast to the very flat-looking front walls of Georgian houses. These embellishments were developed further by the Edwardians who, taking advantage of better personal transport within towns and cities, were able to design houses on wider plots than the Victorians, so that they could include more spacious staircases and embellish them with features such as leaded lights in windows and plenty of other embellishments. After the First World War, houses took on an art deco feel in some areas, perhaps as a

deliberate effort to look towards the future, and in others, the post-war semi-detached house became a watered-down version of the decorative detailing of Edwardian houses. There was also a return to using hinged, side-opening casement windows, as opposed to vertical sliding sash windows introduced by the Georgians and loved by the Victorians, as these had slowly gone out of fashion after a decline that started with the arrival of the Arts and Crafts style at the end of the nineteenth century, which was a reaction against the formality of the Victorian mainstream style of architecture.

Georgian

Medieval houses with timber-framed walls became unfashionable at the beginning of the Georgian period, when brick and symmetry became fashionable; there are many mediaeval houses in the country with later facades, similar to this one.

Georgian buildings favoured formal design with solid walls and sash windows. The ground floor has been made distinctive and more formally impressive by using a different pattern in the stone-work jointing, inspired by the classical orders of ancient Rome, as revived during the Italian Renaissance.

Victorian

This is an example of a medieval house that has had a probably Victorian addition to the left of the house.

The earlier farmhouse to the left is built of the local stone, but has a later addition in brick to the right. The reason for the use of the different materials may relate to the availability of the bricks following the development of the railway network. Bricks may be able to withstand a higher temperature than the local stone, or perhaps were easier to use, accounting for the flue pieced into the stone here.

These are typical Victorian houses with sash windows to all rooms, and a bay window for the main reception room to make it more impressive; the first floor windows have unusual arch headed windows. The roofs have dormer windows in them and substantial chimney-stacks, because nearly every room would have had a coal-burning fireplace instead of the single, large stack often associated with wood fires in mediaeval buildings. The decorative features are factory-made artificial stone used for the bay windows and around the entrance doors. The central keystone in the arch-headed windows is also of artificial stone, as is the horizontal line, just beneath the band of decorative red brick to the first-floor windows. The cornice, which is under the gutter at the junction with the roof, has decorative brackets. This shows how each element is a simple feature by itself, but taken together they make an impressive set of architectural features on a house of this date.

Where taller houses were built it was popular to add a bay window to the first-floor reception rooms, particularly if there were attractive distant views.

This row of cottages has many of the Victorian features, such as slate roofs, chimneys, brick walls and sash windows, but these were less embellished with bay windows, because they were smaller houses.

These houses have first-floor balconies, as well as two-storey bay windows. Decorative brickwork is used around the entrance door and under the eaves at roof level.

Edwardian

Improved transport links enabled houses to be built around the edges of Victorian towns, and this meant that wider plots were able to be used for Edwardian houses. As a result, fashions were able to move away from the Victorian bay window, as wider windows allowed more light into the rooms. The use of casement windows became fashionable again after its use in the Arts and Crafts style that was developed at the end of the Victorian period.

Interwar

As a complete contrast to traditional styles of building, modern houses like these, which have a smooth wall finish and metal windows, became popular between the two World Wars as a change from the more traditional styles of brick- and stone-constructed houses.

Green-glazed tiles like these came in with the Art Deco style in the period between the two World Wars. A forward-looking break with tradition, they remained popular as they gave a Mediterranean feel that recalled the foreign holidays becoming more accessible in the decades after the Second World War.

These houses are typical of the types of designs that were popular during this period.

Semi-detached houses were a popular interwar-type of housing that had developed from the Edwardian period and these made a return to the use of a curved bay window. Though the general style remained popular after the Second World War, features such as bay windows sometimes were omitted in new houses due to shortage of materials.

Individual houses were often quite substantial, even though ceiling heights were lower than in more formal houses of the past. Metal windows became popular, here showing the horizontal emphasis that suited lower rooms.

Italianate Victorian

The Italianate style was used during the early part of the Victorian period, where a typical design feature was the large brackets that were used under the eaves to appear to support the roof.

The pointed arch was the main design feature of the Gothic revival period; the original Gothic period was inspired by a reaction away from the round-headed arch of the early medieval period, but the Victorians also used round arches.

Gothic Victorian

These houses date from the 1840s and give an idea of a Tudor-inspired style that was popular during this period.

Arts and Crafts

This was a change of direction away from the formal and the Gothic and the classically inspired Victorian fashions in architecture back to a more romantic 'vernacular' and informal look. This meant, for example, a move away from vertical sliding sash windows towards side opening casement windows. This style was also an expression of a reaction against Victorian attitudes and developed along with a desire for fresh air, so that conservatories seemed less attractive than open seating areas, such as loggias or covered areas.

This is a design typical of the Arts and Crafts period.

Building Shapes

Single Storey

Early houses were single storey, and this tradition remained a sensible feature in exposed rural areas, to blend with the landscape and avoid damage by the prevailing winds.

The development of a second storey was created by inserting dormer windows into the roof of the house, so that the upper floor could be made habitable, and was not too exposed in areas where there was not much protection from the elements.

Catslide Roofs

This roof goes down to the lower level at the rear of the house and is a useful feature for allowing two storeys at the front of the house and going down to one at the rear.

These types of roof reduced the amount of wall area on a house and are frequently to be found as a result of early extensions.

Mansard Roofs

This is a roof where there are two different slopes on one roof, with the lower one of a steeper pitch than the other. This was a Dutch influence and allowed additional living space within the upper floor, which meant that there was more head-room in these rooms than if a dormer window had been used.

This mansard roof has dormer windows that have been inserted into the roof slopes to allow for habitable rooms to be created in the large roof space.

Part I: Exterior Features

The underlying geology of the United Kingdom is responsible for the great range and variety of building materials that have been available to build houses in this country. They range from building stones that can be used for roofs and walls, to clays that can be fired to make clay tiles for roofs and bricks for walls. In smaller geographical areas there are deposits of slates, which are mainly used for roofs, and granite, which is mainly used for building walls. In addition to materials that are extracted from the ground, there are other materials that grow on the ground such as thatch (which is the unused stems from cereal crops), which can be used for roofs, and trees, which are used for the timber framing of roofs and for walls. Then there are materials such as glass, iron and lead, which are made by processing naturally available raw materials, such as sand, iron and lead ore. These last building products have a high value relative to their bulk, so were worth transporting to areas without the necessary raw materials. The consequence of the availability of this wide range of building materials was that a great variety of different designs and detailing could be created from these initially rather simple materials.

The range of textures and design details that could be created with a little bit of imagination from these simple beginnings are explored in the following chapters on roofs, walls, doors and windows. There are then chapters on other architectural features and a consideration of the general setting of the house.

The materials that are used to make a house look interesting start off as simple materials that are carefully fashioned to make interesting architectural features and design elements for a house.

Chapter 1 Roofs

The main purpose of a roof is to protect the occupants from the elements. Only once the basic functions of shelter had been satisfied could the decorative, rather than purely functional, purposes be considered. The type of materials that were used on roofs depended on what was naturally available in the locality or, later, which could be reasonably transported by river or sea and in combination with a horse and cart. It was only with the establishment of the canal network in the mid-eighteenth century and, a century later, with the development of the railway network, that heavy building materials could be transported much greater distances from their original source. Probably the best example of how a regional building material benefited from the arrival of new methods of long-distance transport was the extensive use of Welsh slates on the roofs of new Victorian houses around the country, once the railway network had been developed.

Slate Roofs

Slate was traditionally used in the areas where it was quarried in Scotland, Cumbria, Wales and Cornwall. These may always have been exported by sea but, once transport links became more flexible with the arrival of the railways, slate could be used almost universally outside its local area of provenance. The distinctive green-coloured Westmoreland slate from Cumbria was able to be transported hundreds of miles by railway for use in London, for example. One reason why grey Welsh slate was so popular for roofing the large number of new houses that were constructed during the Victorian period, was that it could be split easily into large sheets, so a roof could economically be slated with slates of a single size. In addition to which, the scale of the quarrying operations was larger than for other slate quarries in the country.

Slate roofs are typically made from grey-coloured slates in large parts of the country, such as these Welsh slates that were most widespread in their use throughout the country.

This roof has small Scottish slates, because the slates could not be cut into larger sheets, as they broke into smaller pieces and the smallest pieces were accommodated further up the roof slope for economy, saving the larger, and more water-proofing, slates for use at the eaves, where a greater volume of water is present.

A roof that is covered in green-coloured slates often indicates that they are Westmoreland slates from Cumbria.

This gives an idea of the amount of slate that was extracted over the years from this now disused Scottish quarry.

Westmoreland slates are quite thick by comparison with Welsh slates.

Cornish slates have a distinctive character and are used extensively in the local area.

Some types of slates were produced in a range of sizes, depending upon the original size of the block of slate from which they were split; they usually have nail holes on either side of the slate for fixing to the roof using nails and they usually have a pair of nail holes either at the top or near the centre.

This Edwardian house is a typical example of how decorative slates were used to make the roof a more decorative feature.

Slates with decorative edges, as used on this roof, were more expensive to chip into shape, so they were often used in combination with less expensive, plane-edged slates to create a decorative pattern.

Where the slates available ranged in size, smaller slates were used at the head of the roof, with larger ones at the bottom to make use of all the slates; this pattern of laying slates is called diminishing courses. The benefits of having fewer rows of slates at the bottom of a roof, where there is more water running down the roof, means that there are fewer junctions for the water to get into the roof.

Slates could be cut into different shapes on the bottom edges to create interesting patterns within a single roof. Welsh slates, being thinner, larger and easier to trim were more suited to this treatment.

These Cornish slates make a distinctive roof and show how they fitted in with the local landscape.

This slate roof incorporates a shallower pitch at the eaves, which helps to reduce the speed of the water running off the roof.

Clay Roof-Tiles

Clay roof-tiles are historically used where there are clay deposits beneath the surface of the soil that can be made into tiles and fired in a kiln. In some areas, such as the east coast and around various ports, roof tiles, in particular the distinctive pantiles, were imported from abroad centuries ago as ballast on returning trading ships. The overall colour of the clay tiles varies depending on the colour of the clay that was available in a particular locality. However, even after the tiles had been fired, there would also be a variation in the range of colours within each batch of tiles. Tiles nearer to the centre of the kiln and closest to the heat source could be more burnt, and therefore darker in colour, than those that had been stacked further away from the fire. Tiles could also be very slightly different in size, according to the speed and intensity of its firing.

Clay Plain and Peg tiles

The standard size of this simple flat tile was decreed by statute, at $10\frac{1}{2} \times 6\frac{1}{4} \times \frac{5}{8}$in, at various times from the fifteenth to the eighteenth centuries, though not always obeyed. This meant, in theory, that tiles could be interchangeable anywhere in the country. The demand that was created during the Industrial Revolution for new building materials could be met by improved methods of transportation, so that building materials could be transported to outside their traditionally local areas of use. This resulted in a much greater variety of building materials being used on houses all over the country. This did also, however, mean that there was also a reduction in the amount of regional or vernacular building materials that were used locally, with the rise of industrial building processes.

Clay tiles range in colour, depending on where the clay that was used for them was dug from, but generally they range in colour from orange to red, unless some other additives have been mixed in with the clay or a coating has been applied to the tiles before firing to alter the natural colour.

Tiles that have been made in different parts of the county take on a different colour, depending upon the clays and additives that have been used during their manufacturing process.

A row of clay tiled roofs makes an interesting skyline and the subtle variation in the colour of the tiles makes them look interesting.

Where tiles have all been laid at the same date, they weather in a similar way to each other.

As a general rule of thumb, a tile that has holes in it, referred to as a peg tile, is usually older and often hand-made; whereas tiles that have 'nibs' moulded into the top of the tile are often machine-made and are, therefore, usually more recent, mass-produced tiles. The difference between a hand-made tile and a machine-made tile can usually be seen from the appearance of the tile. If there are a series of lines within the tile, this shows where the clay may have been thrown into the tile mould, like throwing dough into a bread tin mould. The more industrialized process for making machine-made tiles is that clay is extruded into a tile mould, which is more like squeezing toothpaste from a tube.

Peg tiles have two holes in the top of the tile, from which they are hung over the roofing battens, using either nails or timber pegs, hence their name 'peg tiles'.

This shows the underside of a clay 'peg' tile roof, where a timber peg is used to hang the tile from the horizontal timber battens that are fixed between the upright roof trusses.

In this picture there are some earlier peg tiles laid upside down, as the twin peg holes at the top of each tile are exposed along the bottom edge of the tiles. As it is difficult to re-hole a tile, they may now be fixed in place with a lime mortar, which can wash away in time. The reason for turning tiles upside down would be that the original bottom edge had become worn and water would have run into the roof space rather than run off the tiles. The reason these tiles were re-used is likely to have been that similar matching tiles were not available, or too expensive, when the roof was being relaid. A tile with one or two holes at the top is a 'peg tile'. These tiles were so called because a timber peg, which was slightly conical in shape, was inserted through the hole in the tile from the outside, so that it was wedged in position at right angles to the tile. The timber peg could then be hung over the timber roofing batten that ran horizontally across a roof slope. These horizontal roofing battens were usually fixed to the roof trusses that make the pitch of the roof. A problem with using timber pegs, even if they are made of oak, which is a durable timber, is that they can shrink or decay. When machine-made iron nails became available, they were widely adopted for roofing, as they were easier to obtain than individually shaped oak pegs; but iron can also decay, so nowadays alloy nails are used.

These are twentieth-century machine-made nibbed plain tiles, here with three nibs at the top of the tiles, as older ones often only have two nibs. These tiles also have two nail holes, which can also be used to nail tiles in place as an added precaution on exposed edges of roofs.

Decorative clay tiles could easily be made with shaped lower edges or, in other examples, different colours of tiles could be used so that they made patterns. Different colours of tiles were made by using alternative types of clay, so that the natural colours of the clays created the difference in colours.

This shows what timber roofing battens look like after clay tiles have been removed. In this case the timber battens are fixed directly onto the timber boarding, which is in turn fixed onto the roof trusses below.

All the clay tiles on this roof have a curved lower edge that gives an overall effect similar to fish scales.

The bottom edge of clay tiles was probably ideally level when the roof was originally laid, and so any later replacements may be noticeable not only by their slightly different colour, but also by their apparent length, if the nail-hole position is slightly different.

Originally, hand-made tiles were inevitably less than uniform and create a gently varied surface. Then factory-made tiles came along, which were very uniform but which may not be visually suitable for old buildings, which do not have a uniform roof structure to start with. Modern 'hand-made' tiles may come from factories but can manage to be reasonably varied in shape.

Rows of decorative tiles were used in combination with plain-edged tiles, as these were no doubt cheaper, so that a decorative effect is achieved at less overall cost than using decorative tiles over the whole roof.

This roof has decorative clay roof-tiles, which are echoed in the designs for the vertical wall tiles.

Underlays Beneath the Roof Finish

Underlays are a layer of material that is laid between the roof timbers and the roofing material to try to reduce the amount of wind-blown water that may get into the roof space, in certain heavy weather conditions. The earliest types of underlay were natural fibres, such as stems of water reed that were closely packed or woven and laid over the roof timbers before the roof covering was fixed on to the roof timbers. Many other natural materials, such as moss, were also used for this purpose. The type of material used, depended on what natural materials were locally available. Another method of increasing the amount of protection from the weather is a process called torching, which is sometimes used under stone or slate roofs, particularly in out-buildings. This is where a layer of lime mortar is applied to the underside of the tiles to reduce the amount of wind, snow and rain that might be able to get in under the tiles in windy conditions. The early modern equivalent of this was to use black felt, which was popular from the 1950s. Felt was used where an older roof was being re-roofed and it was fixed on top of the roof timbers before the timber battens were attached to them. An underlay is used to create a double layer of protection, so that any water that gets blown up between the roofing tiles is not able to get into the roof space. Recent developments in underlays have lead to a variety of materials of various colours being used. The principal difference is that some, but not all, are intended to be waterproof yet 'breathable', following concerns in both modern and ancient buildings that the old black underlay was restricting ventilation and causing mould growth and decay in roof timbers.

The white colour on the underside of this roof indicates that it is lime mortar torching, which is applied to the underside of the slates to keep driving rain from getting into the roof space.

This newly re-laid stone roof has lime mortar, called torching, applied to the underside of these stone slates.

This shows a roof where there is no underlay beneath the tiling battens and the clay tiles are visible from the interior of the roof.

This is a sheet roofing underlay from the early 1990s, used on a slate roof when it was re-laid.

Clay Pantiles

Pantiles are most commonly found along the east coast of the United Kingdom, and around a few other coastal and river areas that had easy access to ports, such as around the Bristol area. The reason for this was that the earliest pantiles were imported from the Netherlands, before the tradition of making pantiles was widely adopted in the United Kingdom. The typical pantile tends to be a flattened 'S' profile, although double S-shaped tiles and other variations may also be found. Their minimum size of not less than 13½ × 9½ × ½in, was set in the eighteenth century, but variations and incompatibilities within this are inevitable. They are laid in a single layer not only a top-to-bottom overlap, but also a side-to-side lap, which permits them to be waterproof without being laid in several thicknesses. This is compared with peg and plain tiles and slates, where there are at least two layers at any one point on a roof. This means that fewer tiles are used on each roof, which makes pantiles a relatively lightweight and potentially economical roofing material by comparison. One consequence of being a lighter weight building material is that they were sometimes used as a replacement roofing material for where roof timbers had become overstressed. Or, alternatively, they were used to replace thatch without the need to reinforce the roof structure. Like some of the larger sizes of slate, pantiles could be used at particularly shallow angles, though they might be less reliable at such low pitches. This accounts for their use on many out-buildings at shallow pitches, which would be cheaper to build and less critical if they leaked. Rooflights were easily formed in such roofs, where there were no ceilings or underlays under the tiles, by inserting a few pantiles made from glass.

The natural colour of pantiles depends on the colour of the locally available clays that were used to make the tiles. The great majority of these tiles tend to be made from reddish coloured clay, but other colours such as yellowy white pantiles are found in East Anglia. Colours and glazes could also be added to the surface of tiles prior to firing, so that in Norfolk and Suffolk, for example, matt black and black-glazed tiles are often found. In the machine age, blue- and green-glazed tiles briefly became fashionable as part of the Art Deco movement.

A roof of pantiles has a distinctive look and is a lighter weight material than clay tiles, as there are fewer layers of tiles over the whole roof.

Pantiles are laid in vertical rows, so the water runs down the middle of a row of tiles, unlike plain clay tiles that have their joints staggered, so that the water runs over the whole surface of the tiles.

Where any roof has a very steep pitch, it is often likely that it has previously been thatched and that the roof covering has been replaced. Other indicators on a roof that it may originally have been thatched are if there are high ends to the edge of the roof, called gable parapets. This may indicate that a much thicker layer of roofing material had previously been used, which has since been replaced. Another indicator of an earlier change in roofing material may be where there are dormer windows within a roof slope. If the dormer windows look as though they may have had a much thicker layer of thatch around them originally, this too may indicate that the pantiles are a later roof covering.

This close-up shows the typical profile of the traditional S-shaped pantile.

Pantiles are frequently paired with 'Dutch gables'.

The roof of this house is covered with black-glazed pantiles.

This shows the difference in height of the Dutch gable, by comparison with the adjacent pantiled roof.

Roofs may be made from a combination of glazed and natural-coloured pantiles to create a distinctive appearance, as in this case.

The colour of pantiles is determined by the type of clay that the tiles are made from or whether glazes have been applied to the tiles before they were fired, as in this case where a black glaze has been used, as may be frequently found in Norfolk and Suffolk.

There are many variations in the shape that may be found in the design of pantiles; here they have a more shallow S-shape.

These pantiles are flat except for the small ridge that is used to cover the joint with the adjoining tile.

This is a variation of pantile that has a double roll.

This is a close-up of a double pantiled roof.

In the 1930s, green- and blue-glazed roof tiles became fashionable. Those that survive are relatively rare, and should be carefully looked after and protected, as replacements for any damaged tiles might take a little time to find.

Glass pantiles may be found on the roofs of out-buildings. They were used to give some illumination to the interior of these spaces, which were usually open to the roof rafters and so the interior space would benefit from the illumination from outside. Glass pantiles are fairly rare, as many have been broken or damaged over the years, so that any that are found should be carefully looked after.

Glass roof tiles can be laid anywhere on a roof where light is required in the room underneath.

Blue-glazed pantiles were used as an impressive feature on buildings from the 1930s.

Stone Roofing Tiles

Stone roof tiles, or stone slates as they are also called, are principally used in areas of the country where the local building stone could be split by hand into thin enough slabs for it to be laid on roofs. These roofing tiles may either be limestone or sandstone, according to the underlying geology in the area. As a rough guide, such stones found north of a line running between the north of Lincolnshire to the north of the Cotswolds are probably sandstones, while south of this line is where limestones are more usually found; however, there are exceptions, such as Horsham slate sandstones, for example. The sizes of the stone tiles that could be used on a roof, were entirely dependant on the sizes of the pieces of stone that could be extracted from the ground and how easy it was to split them into relatively flat pieces. Some areas produced larger pieces of useable stone than others, which will affect the look of traditional roofs in that area. On all types of roof, in order to reduce wastage, where there was a range of stone-tile sizes: the smaller pieces of stone were used at the top of the roof, and the sizes of each row of stone tiles increased down to the bottom of the roof, where the largest pieces of stone were used. This way of using all the sizes of stone tiles is known as 'diminishing courses' and is based on the idea that the top of the roof has to conduct less water than the bottom, and so fewer joints are desirable at the bottom. In addition, the bottom edge, or eaves, of a roof was often shallower to help reduce the speed of the water running over it. Also, heavier, larger stones would be more stable if laid nearly horizontal, if only held in place by oak pegs.

These are limestone tiles used in Lincolnshire and some of the tiles at the bottom of the roof slope are quite sizable.

These limestone tiles from the Cotswolds are smaller, so more rows are laid on a roof than with other types of stone roofs.

Sandstone tiles are traditionally found in the north-western half of the country and are often identified from the large size of the roofing tiles.

These limestone tiles have been laid with traditional oak pegs fixed through holes that were pierced through the stones.

Stone tiles have to be carefully sorted into tiles of the same length to be used on each row before they are laid on the roof.

This roof shows how the roofing tiles are laid in diminishing courses, with the smaller tiles at the top and the largest at the bottom of the roof.

Individual tiles can range in length and width depending on the type of stone used.

Smaller stone tiles are used at the top of the roof where the water run-off is less and the larger stone tiles are used at the bottom of the roof, where more water passes over the roof, so that there are fewer joints for the water to get in.

This shows how these Purbeck limestone tiles increase in size towards the bottom edges, or eaves, of this roof.

Where stone is the local building material, both roofs and walls are likely to be made of the same stone.

These large sandstone slates are only found in a small area around Horsham in Sussex, which is unusual, as most sandstone slates are found further north in the country.

Houses often relate to their surroundings not only visually but by having been built using the stone, timber and soil that surrounds them.

These large stone slabs are used to roof a house, where they are available, as in this case on the Isle of Man.

Thatch

Thatch was one of the earliest forms of roof covering and is part of an ancient tradition of using plant material to waterproof roofs, which has included heather and turf. The two most numerous surviving thatching traditions in this country use either water reed or long, straw stems, each having a distinct appearance and a different method of deploying the stems. Water reed is strongly associated with parts of East Anglia, such as The Broads, but is also provided by other areas with standing water. Long-straw thatching may at one time have been the predominant roofing material for much of the country, but it is now most in evidence in the southern counties of Britain. Parts of the south-west employ long straw but use it in ways that are similar to water-reed thatching; this is known as combed wheat reed thatching.

The original logic of using thatch was that it was a relatively cheap and available material, local to the building. It was a way of using a virtually free by-product of farming (straw) or an abundant natural resource (reed). But changes in farming practice and pressures on wild, natural habitats have limited the traditional local supplies of thatching material. More recently, the availability of lower cost transport has meant that thatch has been used outside its local area and thatching materials have been imported from other countries, but the current trend is now to try to use materials that have been grown more locally to where they are going to be used, and this is also environmentally sensible. Many regional variations are incorporated into the local style of thatching, and individual thatchers are probably even able to identify the work of other individuals in the area.

While Norfolk reed usually has to be replaced completely each time a roof is re-thatched, long-straw thatch is usually trimmed and over-coated with new layers, so that older houses may still have the original bottom layer of thatch adjacent to the original rafters. Where older layers of thatch still remain, these should be retained in situ as a part of the history of the house. They may even still have the soot staining that goes back hundreds of years to the point when the house had no chimney and no upper floor, which is a valuable archaeological record and a proof of age of the building.

Depending on the local regional variations, some houses have raised ridges, which is the cover over the joint between the roof slopes.

Norfolk reed thatch usually has crisp and angular lines and, as the cut ends of the reeds are tapped up into position to lie at an angle to the roof pitch, so it is mainly the ends of the reeds that are visible, like a pack of drinking straws being tapped on a table at an angle. The edge, or verge, of the roof sees the reeds splayed out, so that they can appear end-on there as well.

Long-straw thatch has a much more shaggy appearance by comparison with Norfolk reed, while it is being laid. When the re-thatching of this roof is complete, the straw along the bottom of the roof will be cut to a level edge, in a similar way to which it has already been cut around the dormer window. In addition, liggers, which are hazel strips, are used to secure the side and bottom edges of the straw in place. These features are a way of distinguishing a long-straw roof from a combed-wheat reed roof, which does not have these features.

To keep the ridge at the top of the roof, and the gables (which are the ends) and the eaves at the bottom of the roof in place, lengths of hazel stitching, called liggers, are used in often decorative patterns, with long-straw thatch, to secure these parts of the roof.

On this house the ridge is continuous with the slope of the roof below; this is made possible by the thatching material – straw in this case – being pliable enough to bend over the ridge.

Some areas of the country have used a tradition of 'combed-wheat reed', which is where straw thatching is used in a style similar to that of water-reed thatching. From a distance, combed-wheat reed looks very similar to Norfolk reed thatching, but wheat reed is generally used more in the south-west of the country.

Decorative details are incorporated into the design of this ridge, at the top of this roof, and the hazel strips, called liggers, which are necessary to secure the edges in place, make a decorative pattern.

The decoration on a ridge can be quite ornate, as on this roof, in order to retain the ridge in position.

This ridge detail shows how a decorative pattern is used to secure the ridge in place. With a roof of Norfolk reed, as here, the reed is too brittle to bend over and use for the ridge, so sedge is often used, making a separate ridge necessary.

Ridges tend to have to be re-coated or replaced more often than the sloping areas of thatch, to ensure that water does not get into the thatch below, which it is meant to be protecting.

The design of the roof and ridge varies, depending on the type of materials used and the styles used in the locality.

Thatch may be used on any style of house, providing that the pitch of the roof is steep enough for water to run off the thatch, otherwise the water would lay in the thatch and slowly rot it over time.

Other Roofing Materials

This roof is covered in sheets of zinc, which is often confused with lead, as they look very similar from a distance. Zinc is a thin, rigid, sheet material, which is not so easy to shape as lead, and which has not been as popular a roofing material in Britain, as in some other European countries.

Corrugated iron was developed in the mid-nineteenth century, a product of the new factories of the time, and was often used for cladding the roofs and walls of church halls because it was cheap and easy to build with. It was also used as a cheap, replacement roof-covering, where existing thatch had started to decay or, occasionally, to cover up thatch where sparks from new industrial processes or the coal-powered railways were proving too much of a risk.

A typical use of lead was at the junction between two roof slopes, to stop water getting under the slates. In this case, the lead is fixed to a timber roll, which creates an architectural detail, as well as being a means of fixing the lead in position.

Corrugated iron has been used as the roofing material on the left side of these two cottages, which may originally have been thatched because the left end-wall is higher and at a different angle to the current roof pitch.

Lead is a flexible, formable material and is traditionally used to form junctions between different types of building materials, in order to stop water getting into the gaps. It is also used to cover the junction over changes of direction of roofing materials, such as with slate roofs in this example. Lead was also used for complete flat roofs, but as it has always tended to be an expensive building material, it was used sparingly in these situations on most buildings.

Lead is traditionally used to cover the joint between a wall and an adjoining roof slope with a 'stepped flashing', which is where the lead is bent over and placed in the horizontal brickwork joint. This joint is then filled with mortar to ensure that this feature is watertight.

Thin, lightweight roofing materials, such as fibre-reinforced bitumen, felt and asbestos cement, have competed with natural slate for some time.

Timber shingles expand and contract with the weather, as they absorb water during the winter and dry out during the summer.

Timber shingles are fairly rare and many roofs, where shingles were originally used, have decayed and been replaced by other materials. So, finding a roof made of shingles is rare in this county, mainly due to the damp climate, which rots the timber over time, unlike Scandinavian countries where timber shingles are popular, because the climate is more suitable to this type of construction.

This shows how the corner detail of a timber shingle roof can be created.

Chimneys

The purpose of a chimney is to ensure that smoke is taken away from the structure and occupants of the house. For this reason, chimney-stacks are usually quite tall. Because they form a significant part of the appearance of the house, where funds were available, they were often designed to enhance the overall architectural appearance of the house. Moulded bricks were sometimes used to make decorative chimneys and clay chimney-pots could be added on top of the chimney-stacks. These were produced in a variety of colours and styles, once industrialized processes of manufacture had been developed from the mid-Victorian period onwards, when the railway network was available to transport these pots far and wide around the country. The use of coal as a fuel became possible once the transportation network was developed and, because a coal fire needed slightly different conditions to burn than timber did, taller chimneys were sometimes felt to be necessary. This is why clay chimney-pots were developed in designs hoped to increase the 'draw', once the mechanized manufacturing processes were available to produce them and transport them around the country. The type of pots ranged in design and could be a significant architectural feature to the skyline of a Victorian house.

Simple chimney-stacks were used for kitchen areas to the rear of houses, as in this case to the right side of this roof, while decorative chimney-stacks were used on the front of the house, where they were more visible.

Stone was used for chimney-stacks, where this was the locally available building material.

Chimney-stacks and their pots can become a dominant architectural feature in a row of houses from the Victorian period onwards, as each room tended to have its own fireplace and hence its own flue, so chimney-stacks were a substantial element of a house. Popular colours were red and cream for chimney-pots.

In areas where slate was a local building material, such as Cumbria and Cornwall, two slates would be placed together to form an A-shaped tent-like cover over the top of the chimney flue to stop rainwater from getting into the flue, while still allowing smoke to escape.

These chimney-pots were a popular design, and were designed to help cure smoking chimneys by introducing extra draught.

Simple designs of chimney-pots were used for chimneys to the rear of houses, which were less likely to be seen from the front of the house.

Chimney-pots in various colours became popular once industrialized production and railway transport were available. The type of clay that was used usually determined the colour of the chimney-pot, but with some types of chimney-pots, coloured glazes were used. The silver addition to the right, shows that attempts are still being made to improve and refine the performance of the basic chimney.

The tall chimney-pot on the nearest chimney-stack was designed to draw air up a chimney, where there are other obstructions to wind-flow in the area.

These chimney-pots are designed to help increase the airflow.

Decorative chimneys add interest to a roofline, as with these Victorian versions of Tudor chimneys.

Where the chimney-stack is central in a roof and substantial, it may indicate that the house is medieval in origin, even though the front elevation may be of a later date. Chimney-stacks may have been rebuilt above roof level over the years, and here the chimney has been increased in height, which could be as a result of changing fireplaces to use coal instead of wood.

Decorative brickwork, called 'tumbling', is often used to reduce the size of the chimney flue as it rises up the house.

These six stone chimney-stacks on a Victorian house have been designed to give sufficient height so that additional chimney-pots are not necessary.

This early twentieth-century house allows the chimney to make a significant architectural feature.

A pair of stone chimney-stacks makes an impressive feature on the near roof, while a brick chimney-stack is used on the far roof, with clay chimney-pots on top.

Victorian chimney-stacks sometimes tended to be on the outer walls of houses, unlike medieval houses where the chimney-stack was located in the middle of the house.

A pair of chimney-stacks can add emphasis to the proportions of a single-story house and their height seeks to avoid the extra use of pots.

Chimney-stacks like this make a significant architectural statement about the house, designed at the end of the nineteenth century.

Chimney-stacks were often made of brick, as it was easier to shape around the relatively narrow shapes of the individual flues.

Decorative Roof Details

There are many types of decorative details that are used on roofs to make them look more distinctive and architecturally interesting, once their primary protective function has been met.

Barge-boards are decorative timber boards that are fixed at the edge of roof slopes to protect the ends of the roof from rain being blown up under the edge of the roof covering and into the house. A barge-board is often used in conjunction with a generous overhang of the roof to protect the wall below. Barge-boards that can be seen from the front of the house are often quite decorative by comparison with those at the rear of the house, which are likely to be of a simpler and, therefore, less costly design. The central point of each pitched roof is marked by a vertical timber 'finial'.

Distinctive barge-boards make a very impressive appearance at the front of the house.

This range of Victorian barge-boards displays their decorative features.

The details of the projecting bay window gable are enhanced by a decorative barge-board on this later Victorian house.

The front part of this barge-board is very decorative, while the rear half, to save cost, just gives an outline impression.

Simpler designs of barge-boards are often found at the sides or rear of houses.

Features like these timber finials are often created in Victorian designs for barge-boards.

Eave details below the overhanging roof often have some sort of decorative embellishment, as with these projecting bricks on a Victorian house.

Raised gable ends, like this 'Dutch gable', are features that are used to protect the ends of the roof slope from water penetration, and this was a useful feature to have to protect thatch in windy areas. This raised gable could equally be provided by a straight, gable, parapet wall. The brick or stone wall is built up to above the height of the roof finish, so that the roof abuts it, rather than overlapping it.

On Georgian houses, a dentil course, which is a row of blocks under the cornice, was often used above the windows on the upper floor, to give definition to the top of the house.

The verge, which is the end of a roof, may simply be 'bedded' on top of the wall, as here, with the tiles resting on the wall.

Another popular detail is the use of timber brackets to enhance the appearance of the underside of the eaves.

This shows how brackets can be used, apparently to support the roof on this Victorian house.

The colour of Victorian ridge tiles could be chosen to match or to contrast with the roof below.

These brackets show the range that was used on Victorian houses.

These are a typical design of Victorian ridge tile.

Ridge tiles are used to cover the junction between two roof slopes, so that water is directed away from the joint between them. Clay ridge tiles became popular during the Victorian and Edwardian periods, once they were able to be transported around the country by the railway network.

This is a typical design of plain Victorian ridge tile that was used on slate roofs.

These decorative clay ridge tiles make an interesting addition to the skyline on this Victorian house.

There were many different designs of ridge tiles, but many are lost when buildings are re-roofed.

Ridge details are one of the few elements to stand out during a snowfall.

Decorative finials were often added to the ends of roofs to enhance their appearance.

A hip roof is created where two sloping roofs meet, and this junction has to be protected from the elements. Tiles similar to ridge tiles may be used in these situations.

The junction on this hipped roof, between the two roof slopes, is also covered with a row of plain ridge tiles to make the joint watertight, supported at the bottom by a curled hip-iron.

Specially made clay 'bonnet' tiles were popularly used to cover the hip junction on clay-tiled roofs during the Edwardian period.

Lead is often used to cover the hip junction on slate roofs and is supported on a timber roll mould underneath.

The sloping edges of this roof and the dormer windows are created using bonnet tiles, which are angled to match the roof slopes.

Gutters and downpipes

Gutters became generally popular, once cast iron had been developed during the middle of the nineteenth century. Before that, gutters may have been of timber lined with lead or, alternatively, hidden lead features behind parapets, or simply not used at all, with the roof generously overhanging the walls to throw water clear. Gutters were useful in crowded towns to direct the water into the newly constructed drains of the Victorian period. Besides being a functional element of the house, they can also enhance the architectural appearance.

Decorative features, such as this lion head at the junction between two lengths of guttering, add an interesting architectural detail to this Victorian cast-iron guttering.

The upper section of a rainwater pipe fits loosely inside the lower section of a cast-iron rainwater pipe, which is fixed into the joint between the rows of bricks to avoid damaging the bricks. This design was typical from the Victorian period onwards.

These wrought-iron brackets enhance the architectural appearance of this gutter.

The rainwater from the horizontal cast-iron gutter is discharged into the vertical down pipe, by collecting it in a hopper head at the top of the downpipe. Square-section downpipes were popular during the Victorian period and are an unusual and rare survival.

Hopper heads can be very decorative, as with this design from the Arts and Crafts period.

This splayed hopper head is typical of the Victorian period.

Timber gutters, often lead-lined, were popular before cast iron, but these are now seldom seen.

An alternative way of connecting the cast-iron gutter to the downpipe is by using an angled pipe called a swan neck.

The colour and frequency of rainwater downpipes can have a significant effect on the visual appeal of an elevation, sometimes the effect can be absorbed by the building, while at other times downpipes are used to create formal visual divisions, or they may be hidden around corners.

Chapter 2 Walls

The walling materials in a particular area originally depended on what was available locally. This ranged from timber, where trees were prevalent, to stone walling or clay bricks, depending upon the geology. The use of these regional building materials was limited to the area in which they could reasonably be transported at the time. The earliest form of transport was horse and cart, which could be combined with river and perhaps sea transport, to increase the distances that materials could be transported. Then, with the arrival of the canals in the mid-eighteenth century, these allowed heavier building materials to be transported over greater distances than had previously been possible for inland areas. A further development came with the arrival of the railway network from the mid-nineteenth century, which meant that the previously fairly distinct regional variations in the use of building materials began to become slowly more blurred, as building materials were transported further and further until, by the mid-twentieth century, there was effectively no reason for any difference between building styles in any region of Britain.

Brick

Brick is probably the most popular type of building material in large parts of the country. The colour of the local bricks depended on the colour of the local clay, and ranges from almost black to white in colour. Clay roofing tiles were often made at the same time as bricks were being fired in a kiln and had a similar set of colour ranges. As a general rule, the thinner the brick, the earlier it is in date. Bricks are laid with staggered joints for structural integrity and may be laid in a variety of different bonding patterns. The reason for the different bonding patterns was because the walls were constructed of more than one thickness of brickwork in order to support the upper storeys of the house and the different bonding patterns were ways of securing the bricks together to balance different degrees of strength with appearance and cost of construction.

The majority of bricks in the United Kingdom are usually in the red colour range, but even within this range there are considerable variations in colour.

In the Lake District, where slate is a popular building material, brick is used on the side walls, as the secondary less impressive material. Side walls of houses often show which was considered the cheaper or less fashionable material at the time of construction.

The local bricks are usually of a similar colour in the surrounding area and can be quite distinctive in different parts of the country.

These are white bricks in Oxford.

This house has had a second storey added in Fletton bricks, which are a light-pink colour. These became popular after the Second World War, when bricks were manufactured in large quantities near Peterborough, in Cambridgeshire, for building new houses; so the alterations to this house can be dated to that period, by the type of brick used.

The famous dark yellow/grey London stock bricks came to be made with a certain amount of London's re-used materials, no doubt including a lot of ash, which gave them their distinct colour – an early example of industrial-scale recycling in action.

This is an example of how bricks are laid in a Flemish bond, which is where the shorter side of a brick, called a 'header', is laid next to the long side of the next brick, which is called a 'stretcher', so that a double layer of identical brickwork is laid that is joined together or 'bonded' with every header brick.

These are white bricks in Suffolk.

Here is another example of a brick wall using Flemish bond.

This is a darker coloured brick from South Lincolnshire.

This shows how Flemish bond brickwork looks from a distance. It is traditionally used on the faces of buildings because of its pleasing appearance.

These white bricks are laid in the Flemish bond, but there are also many other brick bonds, such as English bond, which is where one row of headers (the short sides of the bricks) are used in between rows of stretchers (the long sides of bricks). While this creates a structurally strong wall, it does not look so visually pleasing as some other bonds, so this tends not to be used on the main elevation of a house.

Different colours of bricks were used to make the brickwork look more interesting, especially around doors and windows. In this case the grey bricks are laid with only the end of the brick or header visible, and if the wall is only one brick-width deep, these header bricks are snapped in half, so that both ends can be used, hence the term 'snapped header'.

Rat trap bond is an unusual and early form of cavity wall in which the bricks are laid on their side so that the spaces between the bricks create a cavity in between this double row of bricks.

This gives an indication of how different colours of brick can add interest to an elevation by surrounding features like windows and doors in contrasting colours of bricks.

Tuck pointing is where a thin line of white lime putty coloured with sand or stone dust is set into a thicker mortar joint that is coloured to match the surrounding bricks. The reason this technique was used was so that the brickwork gave the impression of being made with very thin white joints and very precise bricks, rather than the more conventional larger joints of standard brickwork that are necessary to compensate for imprecise bricks.

In some cases the tuck pointing may become out of alignment with the actual brick bonding.

Even a small number of contrasting colours of bricks can make an impression on an elevation and relieve an otherwise monotonous surface.

Rows of contrasting red bricks, which are also used over the windows and doors, increase the architectural interest of this elevation.

Alternating colours of rows of bricks change the style of the brickwork, as in this example.

Rows of lighter coloured bricks are used for contrast on this elevation.

Bricks moulded with patterned faces were particularly popular in Victorian times and were often used for decorative effect, as in this vine-leaf detail between the two windows.

Decorative Bricks

Sometimes contrasting brickwork is used to indicate the date that a house was built.

Panels of decorative bricks may be used in combination with contrasting colours of bricks and decorative keystones over the windows to create an interesting elevation.

Diaper Brick Patterns

Diaper brickwork is the name given to contrasting coloured bricks laid to form diamond-shaped patterns within the brickwork, a tradition that was popular from Tudor times. The header or shorter end of the brick was used to create this type of pattern and this may have been a very useful way of using up dark over-burnt bricks to avoid waste. This pattern was revived in Victorian times.

The diaper pattern brickwork between these two houses uses a contrasting light-coloured brick for this pattern, rather than the practice of using over-burnt bricks of the same colour.

Decorative patterns were used to make the most use of all the bricks that were fired in a brick kiln.

Stone

Stone is found in most parts of the country except for East Anglia, which has few really durable building stones. Generally in Scotland and Northern England, sandstones predominate, while in Southern England limestones are more usually found. The dividing line between these two types of stone is roughly along a line between Hull and Bristol. Granite is found in useable quantities in parts of the country, such as northern Scotland, famously around Aberdeen, and also in Cornwall. The technique used for building with stone depended upon the size of the original pieces of stone and whether a smooth face could be made on the surface of the stone. Some types of stone are suitable for having fine features carved into them and Portland stone is often used for carving, for example, while other stones, such as Kentish ragstone, are not so suitable for working to fine detail but may still have been used for general building. In certain parts of the country the available pieces of stone are small, so that local building techniques had to be developed to suit the different types of stone that were available. Where there is a need to repair stone, the most important thing is to identify the specific type of stone that has been used, before any decisions are made as to any new stone that is to be introduced. A useful first point of contact is to speak to the conservation officer at the local authority, who may be able to give advice about the stones used in the local area.

The Craigleith sandstone quarry supplied much of the stone that was used in Edinburgh.

This house is constructed from sandstone in the Yorkshire Dales and larger pieces of stone have been used at the corners of the walls for structural stability.

The Victorian style of architecture owed much to brick and the new artificial stone dressings but could be adapted to use with the local building stone.

Sandstone is used extensively in Yorkshire near to where it is quarried.

Most elements of Victorian architecture could be used in stone buildings.

Some stones are more suited to being dressed into formal courses.

This sandstone from Northamptonshire shows the great range in colours that are available in the United Kingdom.

In a small area of Norfolk there is a very distinctive sandstone called Carstone, but as stone for building is mainly very limited in Norfolk, the brick-making tradition developed more strongly in this area than in other parts of the country.

Contrasting colours of natural materials are created here using a red stone for structural stability at the corner that is adjacent to slate to give an interesting overall effect. This is probably as much for the convenience of construction, as for visual effect or structural durability.

Cotswold limestone is a yellowy cream colour and blends well with the related local stone that is used for the roofing.

Portland limestone is a popular stone from Dorset and its uniform quality and colour have meant that it has been transported widely around the country for finely dressed work. In this case the stone has been shaped into square blocks with a 'rustic' face.

This limestone, used in Oxford, shows the range of colours available in limestone, which does tend to become stained by rain, usually directly underneath any architectural features, where the rainwater runs down the wall below.

This example from Surrey shows some of the range in colours that are available in the United Kingdom, as well as considerable ingenuity here in maximizing the use of irregular stones.

This range of walls and roofs in stone compliment each other and are typical in a stone area.

Materials like chalk may not have been regarded as durable enough by themselves and often need to be contained within another material, such as brick, which can also be used to form precise features and gives a distinctive look to the elevation.

Soft chalk that is used for building walls is often called 'clunch' and is used in areas where chalk is the underlying material beneath the soil, such as around the South Downs in Sussex and parts of East Anglia.

Stone makes an impression when contrasted with bricks for the detailing around windows. The bricks being pre-formed square were probably much easier and cheaper to use than dressing the stone precisely to shape.

Stone Finishes

If a stone is capable of being worked without the face of the stone being chipped away during this process, then the stone can be further dressed in various patterns and finishes, such as the vertical lines on this stone.

This stone has a type of rusticated finish.

This stone has been worked or cut to a very smooth finish, with recesses to accentuate the joints between the blocks. Perfectly square, smooth-faced stone without these deep recesses at the joints would be known as 'ashlar' work. The deep joints seen here are a feature of 'rusticated' masonry, perhaps more usually associated with a textured finish to the face of the stone.

It is very material- and labour-intensive to dress stone perfectly square and all to the same size, and so, for less formal building, stones were roughly dressed and used much more economically.

This Portland stone is able to accept a high level of finish to create architectural details, as seen around the windows.

Slate

Slate is principally used as a roofing material, but where it is the only local stone, it may also be used as a walling material. The largest pieces of slate were used for structural parts of the house, such as for the corners or for the lintels over doors and windows. Smaller pieces of slate were used for the areas of walling in between the larger pieces of slate.

Granite

In parts of Scotland and Cornwall, granite is the predominant building material, which is an extremely hard material; so decorative mouldings, which are difficult to work, are kept to the minimum in most buildings.

At this house in the Lake District, the largest blocks of slate are used in alternating layers at the corners of the house to stitch the courses of slate together and give them structural stability.

This shows the variation in the colours that there can be in a piece of granite.

This wall detail shows how carefully the rows of slates are laid, so that they line through with the larger blocks of slate at the corners, which are staggered in alternating layers.

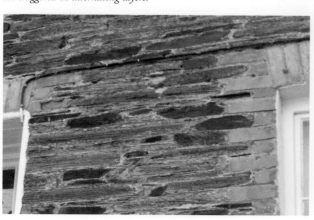

This is an example of slate in Cornwall. The colour and size of the slates contrasts by comparison with that of the Lake District.

This wall of Cornish granite gives an indication the types of architectural features that can be simply created from granite.

Terracotta

This is a material that looks similar to brick, but with additional materials used to create a smoother finish. Terracotta is usually used for feature elements, such as window lintels, door and window surrounds, and became popular during the Victorian period.

This shows how the blocks can be precisely pre-fabricated.

The detailing around the windows is made of terracotta, while bricks are used for the plain walling in between.

Yellow-coloured terracotta was popular for door and window surrounds.

This detail of yellow terracotta over the window shows how it is slotted together with stepped joints.

This shows how terracotta is used around the door and over the windows, in contrast to the surrounding brickwork.

Faience is a glazed form of terracotta and it is rarely seen used on a whole wall.

Earth Wall Construction

There has been a long tradition of building houses out of clays that have not been fired in a kiln, like bricks. There are two main types of unburnt clay building materials in the United Kingdom: 'cob' and 'clay lump' are two of the many regional names for each variant, the names coming from Devon and East Anglia, respectively, though the techniques can be found also in Scotland. The difference between the 'cob' and 'clay lump' types is that the cob type of construction is formed in situ, using a clay-rich earth, usually mixed with straw to bind it, that is allowed to set only once it has been placed in position on a wall, while clay

lump is a two-stage process, in that the clay and the straw reinforcement is shaped using timber moulds to form blocks like large bricks, which are then allowed to dry naturally, before being laid in the same way as brickwork, using a clay-based mortar. The whole of the wall was then covered in layers of earth-based or lime-based render to protect the wall from the elements, while enabling it to 'breathe' out any moisture. This type of construction is particularly sensitive to trapped dampness and unfortunately modern renders and paints have the potential to seal in damp and bring about premature failure.

The clay plaster covering has been removed from this wall to reveal the clay lump blocks from which the wall is constructed.

Wichert, from Buckinghamshire, is a relative of the cob tradition and is made by laying the prepared earth and straw mix in and letting each layer dry, before putting the next on top, which accounts for the visible horizontal lines here. This is a garden wall; a house wall would have been rendered, but it shows the need to have a solid masonry base and a good protective overhang.

This pair of houses, built in the 1920s, are made of clay lump, but often it is only when the external plaster is removed that the type of construction is realized.

Cladding Materials – Tiles, Slates, Render, Weatherboarding, Mock Timbering

There are various materials that have been used as cladding materials, usually to protect the underlying structure of the building, which might be damaged if water was able to gain entry to the fabric, or to cover a timber-framed building. The most popular materials are tiles and slates that are hung on the walls. Render was used as a finishing layer and could be made to look like it was stone, sometimes called stucco. In areas where timber was widespread, it could be used for horizontal strips that are overlapped with one another to create weatherboarding. Where mock or fake-timber framing became popular from the later Victorian period onwards, this was a way of emulating timber-framed buildings from the earlier medieval period.

Tile Hanging

Tile hanging is used in areas where clay tiles are part of the local brick-making tradition. Often straight-edged tiles and tiles with decorative edges could be used in combination with one another to add interest to a wall.

As decorative tiles were more expensive to produce, they were sometimes used with plain tiles to create a more interesting effect. They were often used on the upper storey of a house that was made from timber framing, which is a lighter weight material than a masonry wall, so the tiles are used to protect the wall behind from the elements.

Decorative tiles may be found in many different shapes.

Tile cladding was a popular feature on Edwardian houses and the use of several rows of decorative tiles added interest to the elevation.

Tile hanging was a popular way of adding architectural interest to a wall.

Mathematical tiles are a type of tile that, when hung on the side of a building, looks like bricks. Often they are given away by having been placed on overhanging walls above a timber-framed wall below, as here.

This shows how straight-edged and decorative edged tiles can be used in combination to create and interesting pattern on the elevation.

Slate Hanging

Slate is used in Cornwall as a vertical hanging material, as an additional protection against the elements for exposed walls.

This slate hanging in Cornwall shows the different size of slates that were available for cladding, depending on the locally available slate.

This Cumbrian wall is clad in slate to give added protection from the weather.

Slates may be used as a decorative feature, even though their main purpose may be to protect high-level walls from driving rain. They might be used in situations like this to clad a lightweight timber frame behind.

This is a close-up of the previous picture that shows how the slates are hung on a wall.

Slates were often used to protect the complete wall rather than just specific areas from the weather, depending on their location.

Weatherboarding

Weatherboarding is used to clad timber-framed buildings in areas where timber was more accessible than alternative building materials. Kent and East Anglia display many surviving examples, where the boards are traditionally laid in horizontal rows.

This weatherboarding has a decorative bead-style moulding along the bottom edge of each overlapping board. This seems to have been a nineteenth-century embellishment, as it could make use of machine tools, while earlier centuries made do with straight-edged boards or even waney-edged boards straight from the tree.

Mock-timber framing became fashionable again at the end of the nineteenth century as a revival of the medieval style of building construction.

This house from the early nineteen hundreds has an overhanging first floor that is reminiscent of a medieval timber-framed house.

Many twentieth-century houses used mock-Tudor timber framing for architectural interest.

Weatherboarding became popular for use on new houses at the end of the nineteenth century and at the beginning of the twentieth century. It may also have been used in combination with mock-timber framing, as in this example.

Stucco and Render

Render is a smooth plaster finish applied to the face of the house. The background surface on to which this render was applied could range from timber framing to brick or stonework. Decorative details could be moulded into the plaster finish to give additional decorative features. In some cases, the use of render can turn a timber-framed building into something that looks like stone. Areas with a tradition of timber-framed buildings, which lasted into the nineteenth century, where the timber framing is functional rather than beautiful, may have preferred to render over everything rather than simply infilling between the panels, as had been the mediaeval practice.

This is an example of a Victorian house, with a rendered wall finish.

During the 1930s render was a popular wall covering that was used as a contrast to traditional brick or stonework.

This render has decorative details over the windows called hood moulds that were designed to deflect any water that ran down the face of the wall away from the window on this Victorian house.

Roughcast is a type of render where fine stones or grit are mixed in with the final layer of render, which is then thrown at the wall, while the undercoat of render is still wet. Granite buildings in costal villages were often rendered in order to give added protection against the elements.

Render could be used to create seamless curved walls.

Often the ground floor and lower parts of a house were finished in stucco to give a different visual emphasis to that part of the house. In addition, columns and cornices were also sometimes made from stucco for additional architectural merit.

Stucco is similar to render, but more decorative features are created in the render, often to give the impression of a stone building.

Stucco can be used to create decorative details around the windows or to express architectural features, such as half columns, called pilasters.

Cast stone is a type of render that was cast in moulds, so that the finished components resemble stone.

Typically the ground floors of some Georgian and Victorian houses were often covered with stucco to imitate stone.

The bay window is made from cast stone that was used to resemble stone, so that it contrasted against the adjoining brick.

Many decorative features were available in cast stone during the Victorian period.

Individual elements of Victorian and Edwardian houses were made of cast stone and used in combination with bricks to enhance the visual appeal of a house.

Mock-Timber Framing

This was to give the impression of mediaeval timber framing but applied as an external dressing, rather than being used structurally.

The use of timber framing was to give an impression of a different type of construction.

Houses that imitated mediaeval timber-framed houses became popular during the Victorian period as fashions turned from being inspired by formal Gothic buildings, such as cathedrals, towards being inspired by the vernacular buildings of the same historical period, such as manor houses.

These Victorian houses have encompassed the idea of timber framing in their designs.

Timber framing is used for only a part of this house.

Even though mock-timber framing was extremely popular, and sometimes very convincingly executed, even in materials other than wood, not every example from the Victorian and later period is necessarily fake: genuine timber frame has remained an everyday construction method up to the present day, even though it has strong romantic associations with the past.

Sometimes only one element, as with these gable ends, was emphasized with real or mock timber framing.

These features make use of timber framing on the upper floor.

Sometimes just small areas were decorated to enhance the elevation.

The application of timber framing on the upper floor was a popular design element.

Even a small amount of timber framing was used to complete the elevation.

Flint

Building with flint is popular in areas of the country where flints are found, such as East Anglia, coastal and chalk areas, but the flints usually need to be used in conjunction with a more 'formable' material, such as brick, to frame the flints.

Where there are large areas of mortar between flints, little chips of flint, called galletts, are pushed into the mortar to help stop it from cracking, as the cracks would allow water into the fabric of the house.

These flints are used between brick quoins.

These flints have been chipped, or 'knapped', to shape them into squares with a face that exposes their shiny interiors.

Field pebbles, 'raw' (un-knapped) flints and beach pebbles might all be used, but need brick to form the precise square corners and openings.

A smooth finish has been created on one face only of these flints to make the flat surface of the wall.

This detail shows how the pebbles are carefully graded to match each other before being laid in a wall.

Architectural Features

The details that may be used on a house range from simple and functional to ornate and purely decorative, depending on the type and style of house on which they are being used.

This house has hood moulds over the door and window to deflect the rain away.

This bracket is used to express support for the beam above the door.

Features such as this cast stone canopy over this entrance door, give an architectural interest to this entrance and wall.

This bracket also helps accentuate, by its contrasting colour, support for the pilaster above.

The use of stone details around the windows combines with the tall, rendered chimneys and sweeping roofs to make an architectural statement on this Arts and Crafts house at the beginning of the twentieth century.

The simple stone bracket can be an elegant expression of its structural purpose.

The changes in the roof levels and details give this row of houses an architectural interest.

Arch-headed windows and the details above and around the window add interest to this Victorian house.

The cast stone features around the windows on these Victorian houses gives architectural interest to these Tudor inspired houses.

Features like these arches over the windows of this Victorian house are an unusual and interesting addition to the elevation.

These doors and windows have been emphasized by the details above the door and windows of these Victorian houses, which also have decorative bands of contrasting bricks on the upper floor.

The overall effect of the arches on these windows makes this house much more distinctive.

Attractive architectural features may be created by using bricks in different planes to create decorative features. However, three-dimensional effects rely on strong sun to show them to best advantage and may collect too much rain and snow, so British buildings have also favoured two-dimensional decoration using different-coloured bricks.

A combination of metalwork around the balcony, stained glass and render create interesting architectural details on this Victorian house.

Architectural features may be created out of necessity, as here with the use of an overhanging roof adjacent to the entrance door.

Simple details, as on these houses, can be created by different colours of bricks around the windows and doors, together with a decorative plaque above the doors.

The classically-inspired detail of this stone door surround makes this into an interesting feature on this house and is no doubt intended to invoke thoughts of Ancient Rome.

These details around the fanlight of this Georgian door add interest to the entrance.

These arches create the effect of arched windows, even though the sash windows have straight tops.

A detail over the head of a window like this can add interest, while being a legitimate structural component.

The corner stones and the horizontal bands create interest in this Georgian house and perhaps help to play up the importance of the principal floors, in the manner of the Renaissance style upon which Georgian architecture was based.

This detail of a fern on a Victorian house added interest to the entrance, probably playing on contemporary interest in botanical science.

This exotic balcony and window, dated 1888, add extra interest to this elevation and may have been inspired by thoughts of Empire.

Windows have been used in the chimney-stack to add interest to the elevation of these twentieth-century houses.

Words and Numbers on Houses

Some houses have their names incorporated within the architectural detail of the house.

Name plaques were a popular way of identifying houses.

This name is inscribed in the artificial stone lintel over the entrance.

The name of the house was often applied to the fanlight over the door, using gold leaf inside the glass, from the Victorian period onwards.

A name plaque on a pair of houses indicates the pride taken in constructing houses.

The name or number of a house was often incorporated in the stained glass fanlight above the entrance door; this is particularly effective when lit at night.

Numbers plates like these make an attractive addition to a house.

House numbers were probably unimportant until the postal service, but have been taken up with enthusiasm since.

These numbers are an unusual survival.

The number has been carved into the stone on the entrance to the house.

Balconies

Balconies became popular as decorative features on houses from the Georgian period onwards.

Balconies were a popular feature that was used on houses to allow occupants access to the fresh air.

The type of design used ranged in decoration, depending on the type of Georgian house, which in this case has a solid base.

This row of balconies in Edinburgh highlights the architectural interest that they contribute to the elevation.

Balconies were necessary as guard rails, where the open window could be accessible from the room.

The detail of the decorative render around the bay window and the decorative cast iron balcony rail above the window make these interesting features on this Victorian bay window.

Balcony rails like these were popular on Victorian and Edwardian houses.

Fire Marks

Fire marks were located high up on a building for all to see.

Fire marks were metal badges that were applied to the face of a building, so that if there was a fire, the privately-operated fire-engine crew knew that the property was insured with its company and they would be expected to tackle the fire.

A popular format for a fire mark.

A fire mark with an alternative design.

Sundials, Clocks and Weathervanes

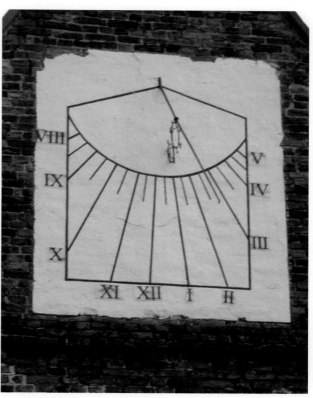

These tend to be found on buildings where there was a reason for time to be important within the household, such as the stables of a country house, or in public places in towns, after the coming of the railway when timetables existed.

Sundials may be found where walls face near south.

Clocks may be found on all types of houses.

Weathervanes tend to be found on out-buildings and may be as decorative or discreet, as the creator of these weathervanes intended.

Coal Holes

Coal had to be delivered and stored before it was used, so cellar storage areas were created either under pavements or directly under the house. The coal was tipped down the hole into the storage area, so where circular plates such as this are seen, this usually indicates where the coal was stored before being taken into the house for use.

This loose piece of stone was found in a garden and shows the coal hole that is now missing its cast iron cover.

This shows where the area under the pavement was used for coal storage.

Later coal-hole plates could be of simple designs, while older coal-hole plates may have the name of the manufacturer on it, in the same ways that manhole covers or toilet cisterns also had the manufacturer's name on them. A round lid was practical because, unlike a square or rectangular one, it is impossible to drop the lid through the frame into the cellar.

This shows where a coal-hole chute is located in a cellar, with the pipes from a later form of heating now located in front of the chute.

Boot Scrapers

Boot scrapers are often seen inserted into the wall of a house near the front door from the Georgian period onwards. This one is made of cast iron. They were more than just decorative at a time before most roads were paved and horses were plentiful.

There were many variations in the design of boot scrapers, with this Gothically inspired Victorian boot-scraper, having a pointed-arch head.

Where there was no way of incorporating a boot scraper elsewhere, ones like this were set into a solid base, so that they could be used by anyone arriving at the house.

Boot scrapers were sometimes incorporated into cast-iron railings, as in this Edwardian example.

This shows a boot scraper incorporated into the stay that keeps the cast-iron railings fixed in location on these Edwardian railings.

Another design of Edwardian boot-scraper incorporated into the gatepost.

Functional Wall Features – Wall Ties, Air Vents and Damp-Proof Courses

Tie bars are traditionally used as a remedy when a building begins to spread. They are long iron rods that tie elements of the structure together and may even cross a house completely. If the ends penetrate a masonry outside wall to restrain it, or to take support from it, then a spreader plate becomes necessary. Their design takes many forms, depending on their location and the available designs, but the 'X' and the 'S' were popular and were simple designs that could be made from wrought iron by a village blacksmith or, later in history, as cast-iron 'off-the-shelf' items from a local foundry. The round plates tend only to be cast iron.

This is a typical S-shaped design for the tie-bar spreader plate.

This is a circular design for the spreader plate.

The tie rod is fixed to the mid-point of the S and then pulled tight.

This shows the design that could be incorporated on the end of a cast-iron spreader plate for a tie bar.

Air vents, mainly of iron or terracotta and sized to equal a brick course, are set within walls to allow air to circulate under timber floors within the house. This helps avoid a build up of moisture, which can lead to decay in the timberwork. They should be kept clear of debris to allow them to function.

This gives an idea of the size of underfloor area that the air vents might be keeping dry, so these should also be kept free of debris to ensure that air circulates freely.

Decorative cast-iron air vents are more likely to be found on the front of the house, whereas simpler designs may be found at the rear of the house. These were used to ventilate the space under the timber floor on the interior.

This air brick is the size of an existing brick.

Air vents are usually made to fit brick coursing sizes and this one is made of cast iron.

Damp-proof courses of two rows of slates were used by the Victorians to keep moisture from rising up into the walls of the house.

Air vents were also made of clay. This is a typical decorative pattern.

Where there are plastic plugs or filled holes in a wall, this indicates that a modern, chemical, damp-proof course has been injected into the wall. In this case, this has been installed just above the line of the slate damp-proof course, which is covered by a thicker mortar joint just below the two rows of plastic plugs.

Chapter 3 Doors and Door Surrounds

Entrance doors and their surrounds give an idea of status and function, so that the main entrance has a more impressive doorway to guide visitors to it, unlike doors to the rear of the house, which would be of a much simpler design. From Georgian times in Britain, inspiration was often drawn from the classical proportions that governed Greek and Roman temple design and which also influenced the Italian Renaissance. British designers and builders took what they wanted from this style without always reproducing its mathematical rules faithfully.

This Georgian timber door-surround has decorative pilasters incorporated into its design and the door has discreet bead mouldings around each panel, so that the central panels are almost continuous with the framing elements of the door.

This Georgian house has a distinctive entrance door that leaves visitors in no doubt about the way in.

This Georgian door-surround has panelled sides to the entrance that have timber raised and fielded panels. These are panels where the central panel is on the same plane as the outer timber. This also seems to have been designed originally to upstage its neighbours.

This Georgian timber door-surround has a fanlight over the door and decorative brackets to support the top of the door surround. The door has four panels that are slightly recessed.

This door surround has been allowed to expand to better follow classical proportions.

This Georgian door-surround has a decorative mould around the edge of the door surround that is enlarged at the base to give the appearance of solidity. The door is a six-panel, raised and fielded panelled door, which is where the panels are on the same plane as the frame of the door.

This timber door-surround incorporates an arch-headed fanlight within the pediment over the door.

This Georgian door has a pitched pediment over it, with dentils on the lower edge and classical architectural details around the column heads. The door has six panels and a glass fanlight over the top of the door. It has adopted classical detail but its elongated shape has taken precedence over strict classical proportions.

An arch-headed Georgian stone door-surround with springing blocks to support the arch.

If there was the opportunity to introduce steps to raise the door, that would give the entrance additional prominence.

This pedimented door-surround is made from stone.

This pair of doors has reeded or fluted detailing to the timber mouldings around each door, which has six panels, of which the top two are glazed to allow light into the entrance hall behind, and the lower four are of a raised and fielded design.

This Gothic-inspired Victorian stone door-surround recalls the Tudor period, with its flattened arch over the door and the vertical boards on the door with face fixed-hinges, creating a distinctive style.

This arch-headed entrance door also has a keystone at the head of the door surround.

For a door surround to stand out from the wall, the design and details may be different to achieve this effect.

The dressed stone used for this door surround contrasts with the random stone used for the walls.

Where the local building material is brick, the door surround may be made of a different material: stone, as here, or painted timber or render, for example, to contrast with the surrounding brickwork.

Here a symmetrical formal design uses two contrasting colours of materials.

Decorative details incorporated into the brickwork mouldings around this door are effective at indicating where the entrance door is located, in this Gothic-inspired door-surround, even if the door itself is not Gothic-inspired.

This decoratively moulded brick doorway has been used to contrast with the walls.

Moulded bricks over this doorway have been used to create a classically inspired pediment entrance on these Edwardian houses.

These two adjoining Victorian houses show how different materials, brick on the left and cast stone on the right, can be used to create different styles of architecture with two almost identical house plans.

While the colour of a door can indicate where the entrance is, this Victorian door uses different colour combinations for the surrounding bricks and stones to create the architecture.

A classically inspired door surround like this Georgian one, with a pedimented head, indicates where the entrance door is located.

A boarded door to a cottage has been given extra presence by some decorative render-work around the door.

The entrance to these houses uses contrasting materials to the surrounding walls.

This Victorian door-surround, which is made from cast stone and has been painted, also has decorative leaves used for the heads of the columns and there is a glass fanlight above the door to illuminate the interior of the entrance porch. The upper panels are framed in 'bolection moulding' – a favourite with the Victorians.

This entrance door-surround is used in combination with the window above on this house from the early part of the twentieth century.

Doors

The style of door that is used on a house, as with door surrounds, indicates the impression that it is intended to give to visitors. Historically, doors in their simplest form, were planks of timber joined together to form a protective barrier against the elements and intruders. The development of panelled doors was a refinement of boarded doors, so that manageable sections of timber could be assembled to create a formal-looking door. The standard door pattern of four panels could be adapted to incorporate more panels and more decorative mouldings, which would also add to the cost of the construction of the door. It was only during the early decades of the twentieth century that stable, manufactured boards, such as plywood, became available to make doors. At first they allowed panels to be both tall and wide, so decreasing them from, say, four to two per door. Later, whole doors ('flush' doors) could be faced with single sheets of plywood over a light timber frame.

Decorative details on this nineteenth-century Gothic-revival door give it an imposing architectural presence, which says to the visitor that there was no expense to be spared here.

A popular design of door with the Victorians, here within a more classically-inspired surround.

This pair of double doors from the nineteenth century has bold, timber mouldings around the panels of each door. The openings for letterboxes were cut into existing doors, usually during the early nineteenth century once the postal service was established. However, after this date doors were designed so as to accommodate letterboxes.

This is a similar design of door to that at the top of this page, but the type of door surround is very different, which gives an idea of how the surround can have almost as much impact as the door.

Door-Panel Profiles
Panelled doors rely on flat or bevel-edged panels being held around their edges in a slot or rebate in the outer framework of the door. Sometimes the edge of the framework was moulded, sometimes square and sometimes there was an applied decorative moulding to cover the join.

This is a typical Victorian moulding detail around the door panels. This is interesting in that the door has six panels, rather than four, which generally tended to be the standard number.

This six-panel Georgian door has 'raised and fielded' panels, which means that the panels are slotted into the framing elements of the door as it is being made, so there is no need for a moulding to cover the joint between the panel and the frame.

This door has angled panels, which is more unusual.

This door has six flat panels trimmed with a heavy 'bolection' moulding.

Here the joint between the panel and the frame is covered with a 'bolection mould'.

This moulding around the door panels overlaps the outer frame.

This door has six raised and fielded panels.

This door has 'raised and fielded' panels, which simply means that the main surface is as flat and level as possible, while the edges are bevelled to slide into the slot around the frame. Simpler doors can be found where there is no hard-edged distinction between the face and the bevel, as here, but the construction is otherwise similar.

Boarded Doors

This is a typical design of boarded door used for an out-building.

Sometimes it is difficult to tell from the outside whether a door is boarded or panelled, but either way a door is usually only a way of assembling timber in a way that is stable and large enough to fill a doorway securely.

This is a typical design of a boarded door to the back of a house. This type of design was cheaper to produce than panelled doors. Typically, the boards would be attached to two or three horizontal cross-members behind, often with a diagonal brace or two to keep the door square.

This is an example of a framed boarded-door, a step up from a simple boarded-door in that it has frame members to the top and each side, as well as the horizontal and diagonal bracing behind. This design of door tended to identify where the secondary points of entry to the house were located, or they could be used for access to passageways to the rear of a row of houses, rather than being the main entrance to a house.

This door has metal studs that have been used to create a design and they may tell us where the diagonal bracing has been put on the other side. Decorative nails were also used as a protective symbol in a more superstitious distant past.

Stable doors are doors that are cut in half horizontally, so that the top part can be opened independently of the bottom part of the door, allowing the horse to see out without escaping. Versions of this arrangement have been popular in kitchens more recently, to keep animals and children in or out.

Where boarded doors are used as entrance doors, there are usually other indicators, like letterboxes and more elaborate door surrounds, which indicate that this is an entry door, rather than a secondary door to the house.

Boarded doors often play on their associations with a baronial Gothic past.

A simple applied design here turns a plain boarded-door into something a little bit more special.

Door Furniture

Here is an example of a door knocker, which was made in cast iron, brass or bronze and became popular in the Victorian period.

A brass door-knocker may be combined with a letterbox to make an impressive feature on a door.

Here is another example of this type of door knocker, where some of the details are slightly different.

Brass door-pulls are useful to close the door from the outside, as well as being a carefully made decorative feature.

This was a popular type of Victorian letterbox, also available in iron, that was used once the penny post had been created, so older doors may have had new openings cut into them for later letterboxes. Doors are said to have acquired one lock for every hundred years of their life, so it is interesting that this Victorian door seems to have had more than its share!

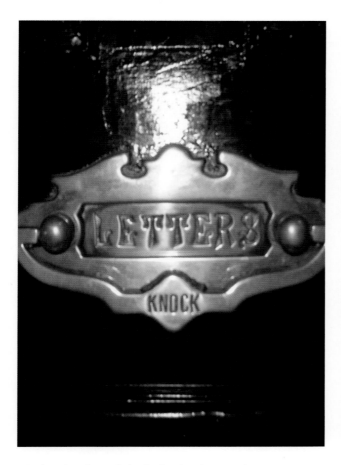

This brass letterbox includes the door knocker in its design.

This brass bell-pull has a square backing plate.

This letterbox is made from cast iron that has slightly different details to the letterbox pictured on page 93.

This Victorian bell-pull is made of cast iron and has decorative details incorporated into the design.

Traditional types of Victorian door-bells are where the middle is pulled outwards, which is connected to a bell wire that rings the bell inside the house.

This bell pull is inset into the stone surround.

This brass bell works by pulling the knob to ring a bell.

This is a cast-iron bell-push surround.

Another design of brass bell-knob that is pulled to ring a bell on the end of a bell wire.

This Victorian door-bell works by pulling the handle to ring the bell inside.

This is a simple design of electric bell-push from the early twentieth century that might be used on a rear door entrance.

This is an example of a typical Victorian latch that was used on the inner face of a boarded door to the rear part of the house, or to storage areas. The thumb latch at the top of the handle is depressed to lift the latch bar on the exterior from its keep.

This is another design of door bell that works by pulling the handle.

This Victorian latch has a decorative, metal, backing plate.

This is an Edwardian example of a latch that was used extensively on boarded doors during the Victorian and Edwardian periods. The latch is opened by lifting the horizontal bar, which has a knob on it for that purpose. The mechanism is based upon a mediaeval timber design (that can still be seen on some old cottages).

An old door-latch and lock-plate cover are a valuable asset to an existing door.

Glass and Doors

The type of glass used in doors has responded to glass-making technology. Hand-blown Georgian glass was called crown glass and was made by blowing a bubble of molten glass and spinning it into a flat circular disk. This was allowed to cool and then square or rectangular pieces of glass could be cut from this glass disk (leaving an unusable 'bulls eye' in the middle that might be sold off cheaply). This type of glass is usually identified by circular lines in a piece of glass. Where the glass is slightly curved in profile, this might indicate that it was made by blowing a cylinder, like a large bottle, and flattening it before trimming into sheets. When industrial production methods were developed, during the Victorian period, obscured glass could be made by laying molten glass on a bed of sand. Factories produced larger sheets than ever before using machinery and rollers to work molten glass, which could be ground flat and polished. This gave a smoother finish to the glass, by comparison with crown glass, but this type of glass does have imperfections in it when compared with modern glass. The Victorians admired patterned and coloured glass, as a result of their love of the mediaeval period, and these decorative glasses, often contained in leaded lights, continued to be popular until the 1930s.

This Georgian door has early 'bulls eye' crown glass in the four panels over the door; they let in light and it was not important here that they distorted the view.

A Georgian glassmaker may not have been proud to have created such a large piece of waste bull's eye but by the mid-twentieth century, such features were much admired and deliberately manufactured.

This is a Victorian example of bull's eye glass.

Industrialized methods of glass production meant that a variety of patterns could be incorporated with the glass, which allowed the privacy of the hall to be retained, while allowing light into the area. Before patterned and cast glasses, ordinary glass was obscured by being acid-etched or 'frosted'.

The upper panels of this door have been glazed with clear glass that has a pattern to make the glass obscure.

Stained glass became popular in the Victorian period, because it allowed light into areas, while retaining the privacy of that area. This example has both patterned and coloured glass, which are joined together with lead cames, which are H-shaped pieces of lead that clasp both sides of the adjacent pieces of glass to join them together.

When illuminated from the interior, stained glass creates an inviting impression of the interior of the house.

Glazed entrance doors incorporating stained glass were popular in the Victorian and Edwardian periods to illuminate the entrance hallway behind.

The different types of glass used, created an interesting design feature in hallways.

The pieces of glass are joined together using pieces of lead, which are soldered together; this leadwork can be a work of art in itself.

The area of stained glass in the door and the framework around the door could make a significant contribution to the amount of natural light in the entrance hall beyond, while still keeping the privacy of the hallway intact.

A typical type design of Edwardian door with stained glass in the door and the fanlight above the door, often included either the house name or number within the design of the stained glass.

This Victorian door has stained glass in the fanlight over the door, as well as in the panels of the door.

The door on the right has been replaced at a later date with a door that incorporates stained glass.

This is a traditional glazed door that allows light into the room behind.

These doors have the upper panels glazed to allow light into the rooms.

This shows how patterned glass is used in an entrance door.

Boarded doors may be made of a few boards, and the joints between boards covered with timber beads.

Doors with Ventilation Screens

The use of grilles in doors was popular where ventilation of the area was important, as well a maintaining the security of the door.

Decoration, as well as security, are incorporated in this door.

Fanlights

Georgian houses had very decorative, curved fanlights over the tops of entrance doors.

The fanlights over these Georgian entrance doors, not only allow light into the hallways behind, but also add to the architectural interest of the elevation.

This door has a glass fanlight that has been covered over.

This is a glass fanlight over the door.

This door has a fanlight with intermediate glazing bars.

This is typical of a square fanlight that was used over the door to the entrance.

Porches

The main purpose of a porch was to protect the entrance door and the occupants from getting wet on arrival at the entrance door. In later times, the porch area was also used as an outdoor seating area and may also have been incorporated with the bay widows on either side of a door.

As well as being practical, a porch draws attention to the entrance.

This Edwardian timber porch has many decorative features to give a distinctive feel to the overall impression of the house.

These are early pre-fabricated metal porches on these Victorian houses.

This porch ensures there is a substantial area to keep the rain off people when they arrive.

Stone lends itself to the sturdy nature of entrance-porch columns, as these Georgian classical-style columns show, with an entrance door that has six panels.

This porch is made from bricks to a design that echoes the adjoining square, bay window.

This Victorian open porch has a decorative barge-board around the eaves.

Details around the entry porch all help to focus on the entrance door.

This Victorian open porch uses a dressed stone as a contrast to the surrounding random stonework on the wall.

This canopy is used as protection against the elements.

A popular design feature in the Victorian period was to incorporate a canopy between the bay windows on either side of an entrance door.

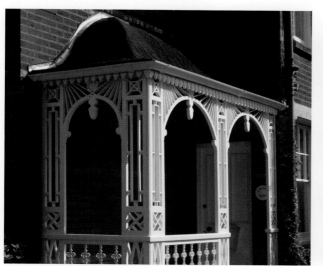

Porches developed into areas where they not only protected visitors from the elements, but were also places to sit and enjoy the fresh air, which was popularized during the Edwardian period, in contrast to the Victorians liking of conservatories.

This close-up shows the projecting brick detail above the canopy roof that adds interest to the upper part of this roof.

This is a more elaborate version of a canopy.

This canopy is of corrugated iron, which gives an interesting detail to this row of Victorian houses.

Using a balcony to double as a canopy was an interesting and popular Edwardian feature.

The detailing of this timber porch creates a distinctive appearance to this house.

This canopy matches the design of the fanlight over the door.

This porch matches the square fanlight over the door.

This curved canopy matches the fanlight of the entry door.

The canopy in its overall setting.

Verandas

Porches are often developed into an architectural feature, as in these nineteenth-century dwellings, where the porch stretches over the bay windows.

Porches were often added at a later date as fashions changed and were used to shade rooms from the sun and to give protection from the weather over the entrance doors.

The Edwardians enjoyed open porches, which were sometimes developed into verandas.

Tiled Entrances

Decorative panels were often used adjacent to entrance doors on later Victorian and Edwardian houses.

The Victorians and Edwardians used tiles in entrance porches for the walls and floors, and there are a number of designs that were popular during this period. These had a practical purpose, where they prevented clothing brushing on the powdery paints of the time.

Hierarchy of Doors

The difference in architectural details indicates which is the main entrance and which is the service entrance.

This pair of Victorian doors indicates the main and the secondary entrance.

Steps and Thresholds

These stone steps, necessary to span the service area beneath, created an imposing entrance to this Georgian house.

Steps were unavoidable where the floor height was above the pavement level.

Steps are easily absorbed into an impressive porch.

Stone was typically used for main entrance-door steps and in many areas the ritual cleaning, with Monday morning's recycled laundry suds, was a social feature.

Decorative floor details were added to enhance the look of the entrance to the house.

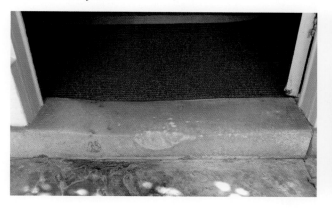

This stone entrance step has seen many years of use.

Patterns were often incorporated into the entry area of a house.

Timber thresholds were used where traffic was lighter.

Decorative tiling and air vents to the cellar are under the stone threshold to the entrance door.

This entrance step is made of a simple slab of stone.

Decorative mosaics were sometimes used in entrance areas.

Chapter 4 Windows

There are a great variety of different types of window that are traditionally found on older houses. In medieval times, the casement window was used, which is where the opening part of the window is hung on hinges at the side and the window usually opens outwards. In the Georgian period, the vertical sliding sash window was developed, where the panels of multi-pane glass that made up the window sashes were hung on sash cords, so that they could slide up and down to open the window. The reason that sash windows were developed during the Georgian period was because of developments in glass manufacture, which led to changes in the architectural fashion of the day. Glass could be blown into larger sheets than was previously available in medieval times and so this allowed the type of window to develop away from the smaller windows of the medieval period. These types of windows became popular on all types of houses, depending on their architectural style. At the end of the nineteenth century, with the arrival of the Arts and Crafts movement, there was a revival in the use of casement windows. This trend was developed during the early to middle part of the twentieth century into a fashion for metal, as well as timber, casement windows, which better suited the lower ceiling heights that were being adopted to save space and money in constructing new houses and flats.

Casement Windows

Casement windows are defined as windows that are hinged at the side of the window and usually open outward. They were popular on houses where sash windows would not be suitable and were used throughout the Georgian and Victorian period on houses where the design of the elevation was more suited to this style of window.

These are examples of late nineteenth-century opening casement windows. Timber glazing bars are used as sub-divisions in each window, so that smaller panes of glass could be used.

These are traditional casement windows and this design, with three vertical windows, was typical of this design suited to low-ceilinged cottages.

This is a typical design of traditional casement windows, with six panes of glass. The opening window to the right has a 'monkey tail' window catch, which is just visible in the middle right-hand pane of glass.

Casement windows could be divided into three smaller panes of glass, as on these later nineteenth-century windows; there is a slightly curved head to the arch above the window.

This type of casement window, from the early twentieth century, had multiple panes of glass. These small-paned windows are used for decorative, rather practical reasons, as larger sheets of glass were available during this period.

These windows from the later nineteenth century are divided into six panes.

These casement windows have decorative upper lights and large panes of glass below, which was a typical detail from the Edwardian period.

Sash Windows

Sash windows usually are made of two vertically movable sliding sashes, hung from sash cords that are balanced in place by sash weights looped over a pulley at the top of the side of the window. The designs are many and varied. Usually there are two equally sized windows, but the upper sash may be smaller in some cases. In some situations one sash may be fixed in place, rather than being a movable part of the window.

The sash frames are on the same plane as the walls.

This shows how early sash windows had the sash frame visible on the elevation.

This is an example of a timber, vertically sliding sash window, which has two sets of glazed sashes with six panes of glass in each sash. These sashes are hung on sash cords, so that they can slide up and down vertically. Earlier timber sash windows had a larger amount of timber around the edges of the windows and it was only with a change in the building regulations of the time, because of fire worries, that later windows had less of the timber surround visible to reduce the risk of fire.

This Victorian example shows how the timber around the edge of the frame is concealed behind the brickwork.

This shows how smaller sash windows were made, with a single row of glazing in each sash.

This shows how different sizes of windows mean that different numbers of glazing bars are used to make the elevation look united. This also shows how the traditional outward opening British casement window would be inconvenient, if opening over a pavement in this position.

Sometimes unequal depths of sash windows were used, as in this case, where the upper sash on the ground floor window is smaller that the bottom sash. One reason why this device was used was the relationship to the internal ceiling height.

These sash windows have six panes of glass in each sash, which was a popular proportion for sash windows.

An unusual practical detail has been incorporated into a sash window.

This is a typical design for Georgian sash windows.

Glazing Bars

This shows a Victorian window that has its original glazing bars.

As the fashions for the design of glazing bars changed, they were moved to the edge of the window to create a border and allow an uninterrupted view through the middle of the window.

During the late-Victorian period there was a fashion for margin lights, which are the narrow strips of glass either side of the larger panes of glass in the main part of the window. This design enabled an uninterrupted view through the centre of the window, making full use of the largest sheets of glass then available.

The use of glazing bars to sub-divide the window sash not only provided structural stability to the sash, but it also meant that smaller sheets of glass, which were less expensive than larger sheets of glass, could be used in the sashes.

The structural stability of the sash window could still be maintained with these glazing bars at the edge of the windows.

Larger sheets of glass were more expensive than smaller sheets in the Victorian period, so they tended to be used on the front of the house, while smaller pieces of glass were used elsewhere.

This shows where glazing bars have been removed on a sash window, when fashions changed and an uninterrupted view through a sash window became a more fashionable priority, enabled by modern sizes of glass.

A fashion developed during the later part of the Victorian period for glazing bars in the upper sash window, while the lower sash had uninterrupted views through the window.

This shows the exterior of the same window where the glazing bars at the sides of the window have been removed, as above.

Sub-divided window sashes meant that smaller and therefore cheaper glass could be put in the upper sash, whereas larger pieces of glass could be used in the bottom sash, where occupants would be looking through them.

Sash Horns

Sash horns are the extended moulded pieces of timber that are used at the corners of larger sash windows that do not have intermediary glazing bars to strengthen the frame for the larger heavy panes of glass. As large sheets of glass were not available until at least 1840, there is less likelihood of horns being found on windows before that date.

The horns were also used on the inner sash as they serve a structural purpose to strengthen the timber joint. Just above the sash horn is the sash cord, which is fixed to the sash at one end and to a balancing weight at the other, which is concealed in the sash box beside the sash window. The inner sash horn is to a simpler design by comparison with that on the exterior.

On some windows the sash horns are the same on both sashes, while on other windows the interior sash horn is less ornate

Sash Cords

This shows a window where the sash cords are being replaced. The sashes can be taken out by removing one side of the internal bead moulding and then putting them back once the sash cords have been renewed.

This sash does not have horns because it has intermediate glazing bars to give the sash strength. It also shows how a sash cord is fixed to the window sashes or, as in this case, the vertical sliding shutter. The sash cord runs over a pulley at the top of the window and is attached to a sash weight of lead or cast iron, which balances the weight of the window sash or the shutter to allow it to move up and down. In this photograph the sash weight has got caught on an edge in the sash box, so it is not keeping the sash cord taught, but by pulling on the sash cord, the weight can usually be freed to run smoothly again, if the sash cord has not broken, in which case it would need to be replaced.

Metal Windows

Metal windows were used as an alternative to timber and many be found on any date of house. The smaller panes of glass within the window frame were usually held together with strips of lead. Iron and steel are stronger than wood and so the frames may be thinner, allowing more of the opening to be glass, which means a better view and lighter rooms.

This window has three lights, with the central one being the opening light. This and the configuration of window below left are not common in older buildings but were enthusiastically adopted by the factory-made twentieth-century standard windows, since they offer a small, secure vent, as well as a large opening sash.

This is a two-light casement window with leaded lights, as above.

The windows that open have a metal frame around them.

This is a more decorative style of cast-iron window frame.

Lead was used to join smaller sections of glass together into larger panels and this technique was revived by the Arts and Crafts style.

Victorian cast-iron window frames had the glazing bars cast within the metal framework, so that the glass had to be cut to fit these usually diamond-shaped openings.

This cast-iron frame includes red glass in the smaller panes of glass.

This is an example of cast iron used for a dormer window.

These metal windows are framed within a stone surround.

Cast-iron windows give this elevation a distinctive look.

These are a typical design of twentieth-century metal windows, which were popular from the interwar period.

The design of these houses makes the most use of these cast-iron windows.

This is a typical design of metal windows from between the wars.

False Windows

False or 'blind' windows were used where it was necessary for the elevation to look balanced in a formal design but this did not fit with the internal plan. Or perhaps later, internal changes have made it necessary to block the window and it is not easy to patch the opening. Sometimes a blind window is simply a recess in the ordinary wall material, but false windows may even have glass and timber sashes in them, even though there is a wall behind them, which is often painted black to further the deception. This device is often used to accommodate the upper part of tall and arch-headed windows, where the window is taller than the ceiling but the tall window has been thought necessary for the architecture of the facade.

Might these false windows be old windows that have been blocked or simply a decorative device?

The pairing of the windows would look different if the false windows had not been designed to add interest to this elevation.

A typical location for false windows is over the main entrance door, where there might be a partition wall between two rooms.

These houses have blind windows painted in over one set of entry doors and not over the other.

This false window maintains the rhythm of the façade.

Glass

The further back in time, the smaller and less optically perfect were the sheets of glass that could be made. The very large sheets of perfectly clear 'float' glass that are available today, contrast with the tiny, uneven squares of glass in mediaeval leaded lights. In between was Georgian hand-blown glass, which was not very large and needed perhaps a dozen sheets in each window but which were cleverly joined together with slender timber frames to create sashes that admitted the maximum amount of light. As technology improved, machine-made glass, formed between rollers or cast and polished, could make sheets large enough to fill a whole window sash by Victorian times. The technology trickled down to provide smaller, cheap sheets of glass for cottage casements that would have been prohibitively expensive a century before. By the interwar period, glass was produced in a range of qualities and sizes applicable to a variety of uses from small, rough panes for greenhouses to large, clear sheets for shop windows and patterned glass had become established not only for privacy but for decoration.

The pane of glass on the left side has been replaced with modern, flat glass, while that on the right displays the general distortion seen with nineteenth-century glass.

The reflections in this window show that each pane is slightly curved, producing an individual reflection and indicating that it may be old hand-made glass.

The refractions through a Georgian window show the different types of glass that have been used in this window over the years. The panes on the left, which have circular lines in them, are 'crown glass', made by spinning molten glass into a circular disc in the Georgian period. The arch-headed pane of glass is modern and it shows no refractions. The lower panes, with a crazed refraction pattern, may come from an intermediate period. Similar distortions would be noticeable outside the building in the reflections in the glass. When placing hand-made glass in a window the glazier would attempt to line the imperfections horizontally to minimize the rippled appearance, noticeable when walking past the window.

Curved glass is rare to find in windows as it was expensive to make, so this Victorian example is a rare survival.

Leaded Lights

The pieces of glass that this method of glass-making produced were fairly small. In order to make up a larger area of glass that was suitable for a small window, smaller pieces of glass were joined together using lead as a jointing material.

Rectangular pieces of glass in leaded lights were a popular design.

This is a typical design of diamond-shaped leaded lights. On the interior is a wrought iron bar to which the lead is tied, so that it does not bow when the lead expands in hot weather.

This is an unusual design for leaded lights that incorporates reproductions of bull's eye glass, which was part of the glass produced when making crown glass.

Patterned Glass

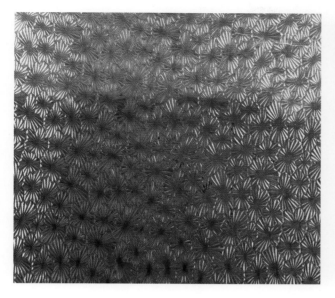

Many types of patterned glass were used in windows and doors during the later nineteenth century and the early twentieth century. This pattern of glass was very popular because it offered a high level of visual privacy, while admitting a good level of light.

This window has perforated, zinc ventilation grills in the top part of the window and patterned glass in the lower part of the window.

This is a type of pressed, patterned, obscured glass from the Victorian period. Some of the older patterns of obscured glass were embossed on both sides for effect, though generally one side would be preferred smooth, so that it was on the outside in order to be more easily cleaned.

This is an example of reeded obscured glass used in these windows.

Coloured Glass

Stained glass was popular in Edwardian windows and particularly in the upper part of the window, where it did not obscure the view out of the window.

This shows how red glass is used to effect in this window.

Types of Windows

The variety of designs that are found on houses depended on their architectural style and the functional purpose.

Splayed Bay Windows
This was an architectural feature used to create a well-lit extra space in a room and which became popular in Victorian times.

This is a typical example of a Victorian bay window.

This bay window uses cast-iron columns to support the brickwork above the window on this Victorian house. Interestingly, many similar bay windows can also be seen near to the route of a local canal, which would probably have been used to transport the columns from the foundry.

This bay window is apparently supported on the timber sash boxes.

This bay window is made from cast artificial stone.

Typically bay windows were used for ground-floor windows in the earlier part of the Victorian period.

This bay window has been painted, but would be cast stone under the paint.

Bay windows could have different designs of brick to create interesting details.

This bay is made from two colours of brick.

These bay windows have been used for the most important room in each house.

Two-storey bay windows became popular later in the Victorian period.

These are two-storey bay windows.

Bay windows were used for the main reception rooms on the ground and first floor, so that upper floors did not need bay windows.

This two-storey bay window has more than the standard three windows.

These two-storey bay windows are supported by cast iron columns.

Square Bay Window

Square bay windows were also a popular Victorian design.

The design of windows could be quite decorative.

These bay windows create a feature to the front of this house.

This double-height bay window has a gable end on top of it for added effect.

Bow and Oriel Windows
The term bow window is often interchangeable with bay window, but a bow window would perhaps be semicircular in plan and be as fully glazed as possible. Oriel describes a small, usually very decorative, projecting bow window, usually placed well above ground-floor level.

These are a typical example of bow windows.

A small high level bow window is often called an oriel window.

Features like this window may be used to give a view from an upper storey.

This oriel window has a feature design below.

This pair of windows is used to give additional views.

This window on the upper floor is supported on brackets.

These windows promise to allow extra light into these rooms.

Dormer Windows

These dormer windows make a significant feature in this row of houses.

Dormer windows allow upper rooms to be useable, where the walls of the house are lower.

Dormer windows allow otherwise uninhabitable areas to be used, as in these Victorian houses.

In Scotland the dormer window was a popular way of increasing the amount of living space, without having to raise the height of the walls in areas where weather conditions and tradition favoured low buildings.

These dormer windows make the attic space much larger.

These dormer windows on a house from the 1920s add to the architectural interest of the house.

Dormer windows are used to allow light into roof spaces, so that habitable rooms can be created within the roof spaces of houses. Their style is usually dependant on the surrounding architecture and the dormer window itself will either have a flat roof or a double-pitched roof from a central point to allow water to run off the roof without creating the necessity for gutters.

Lookout Windows
Where windows are used to make the most of interesting
views they take many forms.

These windows were designed to make the most of distant views from the house.

This window allows for views and seating above the rest of the houses.

This window allows views over the rooftops.

Tower Windows

This house has a variety of different types of rooms that make use of the views.

Turret rooms on the corner of houses were designed to make the most of the view.

This group of houses have a variety of dormer and tower rooms to maximize the use of this view.

A corner room ensured there was the potential for far-reaching views.

This tower window gives views to the sea.

Tripartite Windows
These take many forms from being created within one opening to form three separate openings.

This is a classically inspired arch-headed window, often called a Venetian window.

This is a Victorian version of the Venetian window.

These three-part windows add interest to the elevation.

This is an example of a three-part window.

This Edwardian window is sub-divided into three parts.

Arch-Headed Windows
These windows are popular in all types of architecture.

Arch-headed windows are able to be combined with interesting glazing bar details.

This sash window has a curved stone detail around it.

This window carefully adapts the glazing bars to the overall shape.

These windows, in a style that came to be called 'Gothick', make an impression on this elevation.

This design of window is suitable under a thatched roof.

These pointed 'Gothick' arch-headed windows add drama to this elevation.

Thatch can be used around these types of windows, often referred to as 'eyebrow' windows.

These houses have arch-headed windows that were typical of the Italianate style, which was popular during the Victorian period.

Sliding Windows

Windows that slide side-to-side, rather than up and down, are often referred to as Yorkshire sliding sashes. The advantages of sliding sashes are that they do not require pulley wheels and sash cords, making maintenance simpler.

This is an interesting history of glazing bars on these two horizontal sliding sashes.

This type of window is often called a 'Yorkshire' sliding sash window. The sashes slide open rather than using sash cords and gravity to make them work.

These windows are used within an arch-headed opening.

This shows how the sashes are positioned one behind the other in a sliding sash window.

This sliding sash window also has shutters.

Weavers Windows

Where particularly demanding close work activities, such as weaving, tailoring or sail-making were carried out as much as light as possible was required, and large expanses of window were contrived to be joined together.

Large windows like this indicate that they were used where the amount of light entering the room was important, for work like weaving.

This is another example of a large window.

A window like this may have indicated that it was used for sail-making or other activates that require a high level of natural light.

Unusual Windows

Windows like these have usually been created with a purpose.

Blind Cases

This was a popular window device to give some form of shading or to allow an external blind to be fitted on the exterior of the window.

These types of decorative covers were used in the Victorian period to conceal a fabric blind that was pulled down over the window to keep the sunlight from fading textiles within the room.

This shows a group of three windows where external blinds may have been used.

Window Box Holders

A cast-iron decorative feature was often used to create a place for a window box.

This window has a blind box and a decorative feature that could be used for a window box.

Window Surround Features

These windows give an idea of how the features around the windows of these Victorian houses can create the architecture style of the houses.

Typically, late-Victorian and Edwardian houses had their features framed with a distinctive surrounding to doors and windows.

The use of a white surround to these windows emphasizes these elements on the elevation

The stone around these windows has been designed to emphasize the windows on this wall.

The stone around these windows adds emphasis to this elevation.

The windows on this elevation are framed by bricks of a different colour to emphasize their presence, which was a popular device during the late-Victorian and early Edwardian period.

Window Lintels

Specially made bricks to form the flat arch, called 'voussoirs'.

A semicircular arch enables a structural opening to be made in a masonry wall without a lintel – but that would mean a semicircular opening. So here, a square section has been taken from an arch, which is known as a 'flat arch'. The bricks are angled, as they would be in a semicircular arch, to pass the forces bearing down on them to either side of the opening. These flat arches were often used in conjunction with a timber or iron lintel behind them, which saved using similar elaborate brickwork on the inside wall as well.

Long pieces of slate are used to span across the opening at the top of a window to create the structural lintel over the window. The projecting slate detail over the window is not only a decorative feature, but its purpose is to reduce the amount of driving rain from running down the wall and into the window opening.

External Shutters

These take many forms, depending on the type of house and area. For example, shutters were possible on buildings, once sliding sash windows were in place, so were used from the Georgian period onwards. They once again became popular in the 1910s and 1920s, perhaps influenced by fashions from Empire.

Georgian buildings often had internal shutters in association with the sash boxes that were necessary for vertically sliding sash windows, but here security shutters have been fitted separately outside.

This shows where shutters have been removed, by the staining on the walls.

Shutters may have been original features or may often have been later additions but, if they are longstanding parts of a building's history, then arguably they should be retained.

This row of cottages still retains their shutters.

Internal Shutters

These were a popular way of securing the house from the interior, as well a being a way of keeping the house warmer of an evening.

Internal shutters were popular in the Georgian houses and folded back into shutter boxes at the sides of the window.

Working shutters can be used for privacy like curtains, as well as for security and insulation.

These shutters would open flat against the internal wall of the room. There are also shutters that open into a cavity within the wall, so disappearing completely when open; often these may have been sealed up decades ago and could be brought back into use.

Security

Many types of bars were used on windows, which allowed inward-opening windows to still function.

Bars were used where security was an issue.

Chapter 5 Surrounding the House

The environment around a building has an important impact on its appearance. The factors that can affect the house range from manmade elements like walls and gates to features that change with the seasons, such as trees and plants. Where there is a tree in front of the house, when it is in leaf during the summer it may obscure the front elevation of a house; however, during the winter when the tree loses its leaves, the house will become more visible, so considerations like this are important when thinking about trees and plants around a house, as any change to these can have a significant impact on the setting of a house.

Hedges and plants contribute to the setting of this house.

This gives an idea of how this group of houses looks when the trees are in leaf.

Where evergreen trees and shrubs are located at the front of a house these form a permanent setting for the house.

The same group of houses as in the photograph above are more visible during the winter months, when the trees have lost their leaves.

When these deciduous trees loose their leaves during the winter months, the elevation of the house will be visible.

Hedges can be used to enhance the setting and access to the house.

Decorative brick walls like this make an interesting contribution to the setting.

Hedges can make an impact on the entrance to the house, so keeping them in proportion to the height of the wall will compliment the elevation of the house.

Where a house forms part of a group, the overall setting is important to all the houses, rather than just to the individual house.

The hedges and the arch mirror the elevation of the house.

Plants that are grown on the elevation of a house will change how the house looks; in this case, counteracting the house's intended symmetry.

Any vegetation on a house should be kept well away from the gutter, as has sensibly been done here, so that it does not impede the water flow away from the house.

The type of vegetation on a house can have an impact on how the house looks.

Where creepers have been allowed to wander, they can obscure the architectural features of a house.

Plants used on walls will need to be kept well cut back to ensure windows are not obscured.

Where plants are allowed to grow up walls they may change the architectural appearance of the house.

The setting can make all the difference to the impression that a house makes.

Paths

The type of materials used for entrance paths can influence the appreciation of a house.

These stone slabs encourage a view towards the house.

An informal path is suitable for a cottage garden.

Paths with hard surfaces are useful in winter to avoid the mud and wet weather.

Path Edging

Around established gardens, there may be areas of Victorian path-edging still remaining.

This is another type of Victorian path-edging.

Victorian path-edging, such as this, may sometimes be found overgrown in a garden.

This is another type of Victorian path-edging.

This is another type of Victorian path-edging.

Hard Surfaces

To secure path edging in place, the majority of the tile has to be set below ground for stability, so only the top part is seen above ground.

Cobbles would often date from when horses and carts were used, they helped provide grip for the horses' shoes and were able to withstand the iron tyres of carts.

Where cobbles are still present, they are a part of the history of the surroundings and complement the setting of the house.

Stone steps are a part of the history and fabric of the area.

These stone steps have seen many generations of feet tramping over them.

Where steps are original, as these Edwardian steps, they form part of the historical interest of the house.

Stone steps like these are a part of the surrounding architecture and are often linked to the building of the houses.

Pavements and Paths
While pavements are usually outside the area of responsibility for homeowners, they are linked to the overall appearance of the adjoining houses.

Stone pavements like these form part of the setting for the adjacent houses.

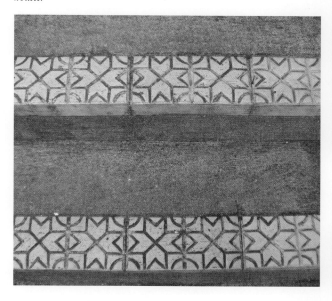

The pattern on these Victorian bricks makes then anti-slip.

These and many other types of block were popular as paving in the Victorian period.

These non-slip Victorian stable blocks were often used where horses might also use the area, so that they did not slip on them; so their presence may also give a clue as to a past function of an area.

These stable blocks have a decorative cast-iron drainage channel in between them to allow water to be taken away from the rainwater pipe at the top of the picture, which would assist avoiding icy patches in winter.

Tiled Paths

During the Victorian period, the fashion for tiled paths became popular once tile-making production became more industrialized. Some designs were made using individually coloured tiles, while others used encaustic tiles – tiles that incorporated more than one colour of clay in the individual tile. As encaustic tiles were more expensive to produce than single-coloured tiles, they tended to be used in combination with plain tiles.

Another variation that uses beige and blue tiles to make the pattern.

This is one of the many variations on this type of design that was popular during the Victorian and Edwardian periods. In this case, the two-tone brown-coloured encaustic tiles are used in the middle and around the edges.

The colours of the tiles in this Victorian tiled path make a distinctive pattern but with only a small two-coloured tile.

This Victorian design uses small beige and red-coloured encaustic tiles in the middle of the pattern and around the edges.

The path often takes its principal colour from the brickwork of the house.

A chequerboard pattern was always easy to achieve with standard tiles.

This Victorian design was used in various parts of the country.

Manhole Covers

Manhole covers were a requirement once drains were laid to houses. This started to happen in towns during the Victorian period. Manhole covers were necessary so that where there is a junction between drains, if there is a blockage at the junction, this can be located. The manhole covers themselves could be pieces of stone or cast-iron covers, which often had the manufacturer's name on them.

Earlier manhole covers that were made locally of cast iron often had the manufacturers name and location cast into the cover.

Stone manhole covers were a way of disguising them in paved areas.

Modern manhole covers tend to be less distinctive, and made from galvanized steel, but do also have anti-slip surfaces on them.

Garden Walls

The type of material used for garden walls depended upon what the locally available building materials were. Garden walls were also useful for using up left-over building materials from the construction of the house. In addition, where any bricks or stones were not able to be used on the house because of their inferior quality, they might be used up on the garden walls. Because there were no waste skips to take building materials away to land-fill sites, most left-over building materials had to be used up in the house or around the garden, which is why some features may have even been created to use up surplus building materials, perhaps also providing a way of training apprentices.

Brick Walls
Bricks tended either to be made especially for the garden walls to create a feature, or they were constructed using surplus bricks from the construction of the house.

These decorative Victorian bricks are used to separate the gardens from the pavement.

Victorian garden walls could be created using different coloured bricks and unusual 'standard special' shapes of bricks.

Low garden walls, using the same type of bricks as the house, were often designed to have hedges grown over the top of them in Victorian times in urban areas, in order to introduce greenery into the urban environment.

This garden wall inventively uses an ordinary building product to advantage.

The covering to the top of a brick wall is called a coping.

Brick walls and timber gates are used to enclose the front gardens of these Victorian houses.

This is an example of a Victorian angled coping to cover the top of the wall.

This garden wall appears to have been constructed from the bricks that were left over from building the house.

This is an usual type of garden wall called a crinkle-crankle wall, which gains its stability from its 'folded' plan form.

Stone Walls
Where stone was the local building material, the walls around the garden were often the places where the remaining stone was used up.

The largest pieces of stone were used for gateposts, so that the wooden gates could be hung on them.

These Victorian stone gateposts have been specially shaped, but the timber gates have been lost, so that all that remains are the hinges on the gateposts.

These Victorian stone gateposts and walls help create the setting for the house beyond.

House names may be hand-carved into gateposts.

Features like this stone add interest to the wall, and often old stone sinks from the house were re-used as garden flower boxes, after they became redundant in the house.

The slate that the front of these Victorian houses is built from is used in the garden walls, while the side wall of the house, that is considered less important, is made of brick.

This shows how courses of long slates are used to bond the wall together.

This wall of carstone in Norfolk makes an interesting addition to the setting of the house.

Because of cost, it is rare to find garden walls of such precisely worked stone.

The tradition of dry stone walling in all parts of the country where stone is the local building material, means that all available stones are used to make the walls. The regional styles of dry stone walling depend on the size and shape of the locally available stones, and are used extensively for field and garden walls in these areas. Each area will have its own traditions of construction.

Dry stone walls are traditionally used around the houses and fields in areas where stone is an abundant local building material.

Flint and Pebble Walls

Pebbles or flints are popular for garden walls in coastal areas where they are plentiful, or even inland where they were once painstakingly removed from arable land.

Flints tend to have to be used within panels of brickwork for stability and in this case some bricks have been mixed in with the flints as well. The wall is covered with a brick coping to keep the rain from getting into the core of the wall and damaging it.

What is good for the house is here also good for the garden wall.

Other Materials
Walls are often made from whatever is left over when a
building project has been completed.

*This modern wall seems to incorporate building materials from a recent building project or
demolition, and so would give a potted history of the site.*

*Hedges are a popular way of introducing colour and vegetation into the front garden of a house
and are also a way of creating a little more privacy from the public footpath.*

Metalwork

Wrought iron was the earliest type of hand-crafted iron; this was followed by the development of cast iron during the Victorian period, which allowed repeated patterns to be cast into moulds.

Entrance Gates

Entrance gates can range from purely functional to deliberately impressive.

These gates show the amount of skill that is used to create an impressive entrance.

This wrought-iron gate has many intricate details that have been made by hammering the wrought iron into shape by hand and would have taken many hours to construct.

These entrance gates were probably bought as a complete set with their cast-iron gateposts.

The lower rails are evidently spaced to keep wildlife out or pets in.

This wrought-iron gate is hung on granite gateposts.

This wrought-iron gate offers some pleasant decoration and this would have helped sell these products.

Some gates that were intended to impress.

Even the fastening devices can be artistic in themselves.

This entrance is defined by finely crafted cast-iron gate piers and wrought-iron gates.

This gatepost appears to be a recycled cast iron bollard.

Railings

Metal railings are used around houses to define the extent of the boundary, and, depending on the design, may also be intended to deter entry. Cast iron is more suited to railings as it is made from a mould that allows repetition, whereas hand-made wrought-iron railings were more costly to make and each bar had to be individually made. In some types of railing, the repetitive decorative elements are made from cast iron, while the bars are made from wrought iron.

Hoop-headed railings are a typical repetitive design from the nineteenth century.

The decorative detail on this wrought-iron gate indicates that each element is individually made and then joined together.

Hooped iron gates were a popular design.

Decorative swirls were individually hammered into shape in wrought iron.

Cast-iron railings were often used in combination with the local building materials to add interest to the setting and balance the costs.

Cast-iron details were popular in the Victorian period.

The base of these railings is fixed to a plate so that they could be supported on a low brick wall.

A row of railings like these have a pleasing effect on this streetscape.

An unusual combination of straight and wavy railings are used here with cast iron posts.

Arrowheads were a popular Victorian design for railings.

These railings are fixed into holes in the stonework below the railings; each pocket would typically have been filled with lead.

This stonework indicates where railings have been removed, which could have happened during the Second World War when material was requisitioned, unfortunately regardless of whether it was suitable for the war effort or not.

These cast-iron railings are complicated and were probably more expensive to manufacture.

These Victorian railing uprights are made from cast iron and used to define the boundary in combination with the iron rails and wall below.

This railing may have been intended to keep debris and dogs out of the area behind the railings, as well as being a decorative feature.

This design of iron railing was popular for defining a boundary on top of a wall, without obscuring the view of the house.

These cast-iron railings have a distinctive pattern.

Repetitive panels are a necessary feature of cast-iron railings, which would be made up from a limited number of standard sections.

This decorative cast-iron gate and railing create an interesting setting for this Victorian house.

This Victorian cast-iron railing has survived despite having lost a few parts over the years. Designs were often specific to a local foundry that would have probably also have made agricultural machinery, and so can be limited to a specific area.

These cast-iron railings make an unusual feature on this boundary.

These ornate railings are a rare example of the level of decoration that was achievable in Victorian railings.

An unusual Victorian set of railings compliment this house.

These railings are designed to be used on top of a low brick wall.

This railing is designed to compliment the design of the house behind and to ensure that light is not restricted from the lower window.

Decorative details in cast iron could be quite impressive.

Theses show the detail that could be incorporated into cast-iron railings.

Railings Around Gardens

This is a fairly typical design of field and boundary fence that was used from the Victorian period onwards.

The design of a garden fence is usually pointed to allow water to run off the top of the timber, but other designs that allow the water to run off are also seen.

Timber Fences and Gates

Timber gates and fences can tend to rot through a lack of maintenance or age, so there may be very few ancient surviving elements.

Timber gates were popular in rural settings.

Garden fences are popular around country cottages and the simplest version, with upright palings, are called picket fences.

Gates may be simple to be effective as entry points to the house.

Unusual gates like this, which are used to keep animals from getting through, are a rare survival.

A good hardwood can be surprisingly durable, though most such timber would benefit from an appropriate natural oil dressing from time to time.

Gate and fences like these are fitting for this type of Victorian house.

Gates like this are a deterrent to animals wandering along the road.

Timber gates tend to rot after a while, so to find the original design like this is rare.

Gates may take many forms and this timber gate is unusual in its survival.

Wooden Vehicular Gates

Gates like this Gothic-inspired gate make a dramatic entrance.

Large timber gates like this are rare as they tend to have rotted over time or have been replaced.

Field Gates

There are many traditional regional designs of field gates in the country, but when they rot, they are often replaced by standardized modern gates.

This gate still has its original stone gateposts.

Gates like this follow the local regional style.

Another example of the same local style of field gate.

Hedges and Plants

Hedges and plants are popular ways of creating an interesting boundary along the front of a house.

Garden and Field Boundaries

Garden boundaries are often defined by whatever materials are most easily available, so hedges were a popular and ideal way to create the boundary between properties.

This hedge matches the height of the gate and does not obscure the views from the house.

Hedges are a natural boundary between gardens.

Hedges and trees that are clipped back each year can enhance the view of a house from the street.

These are substantial stone fence posts.

The setting of a house can be enhanced by the planting in the front garden, as in these Victorian houses.

This shows how a boundary has been created using large stones.

Out-Buildings

Where space is sufficient in a garden, there were opportunities for various buildings in the garden and they tend to range from stables, which were later converted into garages, to earth closets, which were used before bathrooms were introduced into houses.

Garages were often developed from the stables or shed in the garden.

Garage Doors

As motor cars were a twentieth-century invention, older houses where garages now exist may have been used as cart entrances, as the wide and high doors were convenient for both purposes.

Doors were often used to keep the passageway secure.

Doors may have been repaired over the ages, but they are still a part of the history of the house and its garden.

The entrance to the rear of a house was usually gated to keep it secure.

Garage doors often show their age by the number of repairs that they have had in the past, as the bottoms of the doors tend to decay when they come into contact with water.

Decorative doors were used to create an impression on the road frontage.

These are typical cart or later garage doors, with the vertical boarding and a substantial timber frame behind, and large hinges to hold the weight of the doors.

These doors may be twentieth century, but they are a survival in themselves as many of this pattern have since been replaced.

Vertical boards often signify a working entrance.

Open, covered areas may be used as garage spaces.

Archways

Archways were used for access to courtyards at the rear of a property, and rooms over the arch could be created as well.

This archway indicates where the access to the rear of the house may have been used for a horse and cart.

This archway indicates that access to the rear may have been necessary for a high-sided cart.

Other Out-Buildings, Sheds, Earth Closets and Privies

Before the invention of the internal bathroom and its associated plumbing, the earth closet or privy was usually located in the garden.

A privy down the garden was typical in rural areas and glass pantiles on the roof, as shown here, would have allowed a little useful illumination into the space below.

Out-buildings may take many forms – this one has some illumination by means of glass pantiles on the roof.

A lean-to extension at the end of a house often identifies where the privy or water closet was once located before internal plumbing.

The end building on the house was usually where the privy was located, until the arrival of internal bathrooms.

Follies

While follies are a rare feature, they may be found wherever anyone was prepared to put the time and money into building something unusual.

Follies are not necessarily entirely whimsical, since many serve a useful purpose, while also being decorative.

A folly like this makes an impressive entry to the house beyond.

This shows the detail that was made of the entrance gate in the previous picture.

Conservatories

While timber conservatories were popular with the Victorian, relatively few survive in their original form and they tend to rot if not carefully maintained with finishes compatible with their traditional construction. When they went out of fashion, many were demolished.

Timber Victorian conservatories are a rare survival and this one may have had a new roof, whereas the timber windows still survive.

This greenhouse has had a new roof but the end wall and the decorative ridge seem original.

Features

There are many other features that create an interesting setting for a house and they are a part of the history of the locality.

Post boxes are a familiar sight and may be dated by the monogram of the monarch that is cast into the box itself.

This letterbox is an impressive example in this setting.

Water pumps are unnecessary today, but are an interesting survival from the past before the arrival of piped water to individual houses.

Dew ponds are a feature of fields to allow animals a source of water and were lined with clay to ensure they retained water in them.

Part II: Interior Features

The interior features are a very important part of a house, and are often parts of the house that have been lost over the years, when perceived improvements have been made, which may have, in fact, removed or obliterated the original character of the house.

This part of the book covers the interior features of houses starting with ceilings and then moving on to walls and floors, before looking at internal doors and window features. This is followed by a look at individual items such as staircases, fireplaces and architectural features. The functional parts of the house, such as kitchen and bathroom fittings, are then looked at together with the services that are required for a house to function.

Chapter 6 Ceilings, Walls and Floors

The ceilings, walls and floor of a room create a pleasant environment in which to live; their original purpose was to line the cruder structure that keeps the weather out. Once the purely functional purposes had been met, decorative embellishments were added to enhance the appearance for the occupants, as well as, no doubt, to impress visitors.

Ceilings

The original purpose of a ceiling was to keep heat within a room in winter and to stop dirt and dust from dropping through from the floorboards or roof above. The most usual type of surviving traditional ceiling construction, used over the centuries, is one made from timber laths, which are then covered with a layer of wet plaster or render and allowed to dry. The timber laths are nailed onto the underside of the timber floor joists from the room above. These laths are laid close to each other, but not touching, so that when wet plaster, made from lime render reinforced with animal hair, is applied to the timber laths, little hooks of plaster are pushed into the gaps between the laths and over the tops of the laths. This forms a hook over the top of the laths that keeps the plaster securely in place, which could then be built up into several coats to form a smooth surface. The underlying coats of plaster usually had animal hair, such as goat hair, mixed in with the plaster as reinforcement. More recently, in the 1960s and 1970s, patterns were introduced into the ceilings of new houses using new, thin surface coatings on plasterboard, or perhaps these coatings were used as a repair finish to conceal cracks in an existing ceiling.

From about the late 1950s, plasterboard started to be normal for domestic ceilings, which was a factory-made layer of gypsum plaster that was sandwiched between two layers of paper. This rigid board was cut to shape to fit the ceiling, which could then have a thin final coat of gypsum plaster applied to conceal the joints between the sheets of plasterboard. This method became popular because it took less time to finish a ceiling, even though the joints between the boards had to be covered and the surface covered with a thin layer of plaster. Traditionally lime plaster ceilings were painted with distemper, which is a water-based solution made from powdered chalk and a glue size. Each time the ceilings were redecorated, the older layer of distemper could be brushed down or even washed off and a new layer of distemper applied. The benefit of a distemper-finished ceiling is that this finish is breathable, so that any dampness that got into the fabric of the ceiling was able to dry out easily. This meant that a build up of dampness was avoided, helping to avoid decay. Sometimes plain or embossed papers, which became popular in the Victorian period, were applied to the ceiling, which was then decorated. During the 1970s, woodchip paper, which had small chips of wood incorporated into it, to give a textured effect, became popular as it could cover over minor cracks. For this reason it became popular as a remedial finish.

A cornice is a decorative feature that was used to cover the junction between the wall and ceiling in the more important rooms of a house. Cornices tend to be found in hallways and reception rooms, while bedrooms tend to have very plain cornices, if there is any decoration at all, and attics usually do not have such decorative features. Cornices are not usually found in kitchens or in the more functional rooms of a house. In the main entrance hall and reception rooms, ceiling roses were used as a decorative feature, as well as perhaps serving as a way of disguising the smoke blackening from the candles or gas lamps, any smuts might be disguised within the roses' designs and even re-painted separately from the ceiling. The height of ceilings effectively increased from medieval to Georgian times, and then stayed at more or less the same height through the Victorian and Edwardian period, until after the First World War when ceiling heights reduced, which was coupled with a return to using casement windows, rather than sash windows, which tended to require higher ceilings.

This shows where an area of plaster ceiling has fallen down, and the timber laths have been exposed. Where plaster is visible between the timber laths, this is the remains of the hooks of plaster that are lapped over the back of the laths to keep the ceiling in place.

This ceiling has not been painted with limewash or distemper for a number of years and, as a result, the vertical lines of the timber floor joists to which the laths have been fixed are visible through pattern staining where dirt is deposited through condensation on the cooler areas. The horizontal lines are the timber laths, to which the plaster is applied, the vertical lines are the thicker timbers behind.

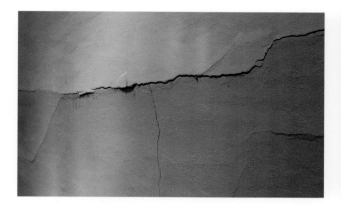

Where cracks 'wobble' across the ceiling like this, it indicates that the ceiling is probably made of lath and plaster.

Embossed papers, which were popular in Victorian and Edwardian houses, like this, were used to give an architectural effect to a flat ceiling.

Where a ceiling in an older house, like this one, has a straight line crack in it, this usually indicates that the ceiling has been replaced with a plasterboard ceiling at some point in the past. One reason why a ceiling might have been replaced is if it was damaged; for example, if a bomb was dropped locally during the Second World War and the vibration broke the keys that kept the old lath and plaster ceiling in place. Water damage from the room or roof above is another reason why ceilings have been replaced in the past. Often the straight edges of a plasterboard ceiling only begin to become visible after a few years, as the boards expand and contract during the seasons and eventually the joint between the boards becomes visible. Sometimes plasterboard, or other modern ceilings, have been applied over old, defective lath and plaster ceilings, which can place too much weight on the new ceiling. There is usually no reason not to explore having a traditional lath and plaster ceiling repaired traditionally, provided it can be done competently. Lath and plaster offers a unique appearance and has some distinct advantages in performance related to older buildings.

Mediaeval ceiling decoration was worked into the wet ceiling lime plaster and built up in layers and 'run' with profiled former templates. Later, similar techniques were applied in plaster of Paris, a more precise material that could be made up into pre-fabricated lengths of cornice and other applied decoration sometimes using wooden formers and hessian reinforcement. The finished article was then cut to size and applied to a finished level ceiling. This was the technique that produced most of the elaborate Victorian and Edwardian cornices, though both skills were present in Georgian building and both still survive today.

There are many different types of paper finish that may have been applied to a plaster ceiling over the years. These are often used to cover over small cracks in the underlying ceiling. One popular type of ceiling paper finish, from the 1960s and 1970s, was woodchip wallpaper. This has small chips of wood embedded into the paper to give it a 'textured' appearance. This was seen as being very useful for disguising any small cracks in the underlying ceiling or walls.

This shows a decorative Victorian cornice, with a picture rail below. Some of the details have started to get clogged by many layers of paint, which is a useful indicator that this is an original cornice, as modern cornices tend to have crisper details, as they have had fewer coats of paint applied to them.

The depth of a cornice was related to the size of this reception room, which dates from the 1890s.

An Edwardian cornice like this would have been run by hand, with layers of plaster being built up in situ until the correct profile was reached all around the room.

This is a late-Victorian cornice in a less public room than the previous example and is less ornate. Unfortunately the picture rail has been partially removed.

Where original cornices have been lost, modern, decorative cornices, as here, are still made in the same way as traditional cornices and can be re-instated. The detailing is usually much clearer, as fewer layers of paint have been applied over the years.

In this Edwardian room, the cornice has been modelled to accommodate the different angles within the room.

To give this room scale, this Victorian cornice has had additional decorative strips and rosettes added on the ceiling area adjacent to the cornice.

Decorative details around the cornice may be original or may sometimes have been added at a later date. A good way of finding this out is to look at the same features in similar types of Victorian or Edwardian houses in the surrounding area.

These decorative plaster brackets in this Victorian entrance hall are a typical nineteenth-century embellishment, together with the picture rail and the dado rail, which is just visible in the background, while in the foreground the architrave of a door is just visible.

This Victorian cornice has had decorative features fixed to the cornice.

This ceiling rose in this Victorian entrance hall still has the stem of the old gas supply pipe for the light fitting in place.

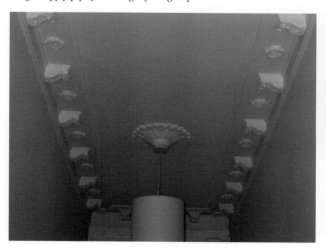

This Victorian entrance hall has a small ceiling rose, as well as decorative brackets and circular motifs applied to the cornices around the walls.

The original purpose of ceiling roses was to protect the rest of the ceiling from staining from the candles or the gas lamps in a central light fitting below the rose. It meant that only the area of the ceiling immediately above the light fitting was discoloured and this was, to a certain extent, disguised by the decorations on the ceiling rose. Ceiling roses were used as a decorative feature in principal rooms of the house to add to the architectural character and status of the room, and tended not always to be found in bedrooms or private rooms on the upper storeys of a house.

The size of the ceiling rose has to be in proportion to the room, so this Victorian ceiling rose gives the impression of being of a larger diameter by having an additional moulding around the edge of the ceiling rose.

The detail of a ceiling rose often gets clogged with distemper when the room is redecorated, so where a ceiling rose still has its original distemper paint finish, if it needs to be re-painted, then by applying some water to the rose, it is possible to remove the distemper, so that the original plasterwork details are revealed. Emulsion paint can be very difficult to remove and should normally be avoided when redecorating such delicate features.

This shows how an extra plaster moulding is used around the edge of a ceiling rose to increase its prominence within the room.

This modern ceiling rose is made using traditional plastering methods and is a replacement for an earlier ceiling rose that has been lost.

This shows the reverse of a modern, but traditionally made, fibrous plaster ceiling rose showing the reinforcement.

Where there is a structural beam that is lower than the surrounding ceiling, this is often covered with a timber boxing, as in this early Edwardian example, which has a bead mould detail at the corners to disguise the straight joint.

This beam was covered in Victorian times by this timber casing and a bead moulding detail has been used at the edges, as well as in the middle where two pieces of timber have been joined together.

Walls

The major vertical elements in a room can be made from, and finished in, a variety of materials, which are then adorned with features like picture rails and skirting boards to make them more interesting and useful. As all internal walls were usually concealed by plaster, the way of identifying a solid masonry wall, which is made of brick or stone, is to tap it to see if it sounds solid all over. If it sounds generally hollow, this means that it is likely to be a timber lath and plaster wall in an older house. These types of walls tended to be used for internal walls on upper floors to reduce the floor loading, but also to act as structural braces for the overall design of the house. Where an external wall on the ground floor sounds hollow all over and the outside wall is of brick or stone, this may mean that a timber framed wall has been used to line the wall. It was rare for internal walls in the post-mediaeval period to be a bare brick or stone finish, this finish was generally only found in out-buildings or perhaps some cottages, where the expense of applying plaster to the walls could not be justified.

Timber panelling was sometimes applied either to the full height of a room or to about half way up the wall, which was then called dado panelling. The architectural features that went in and out of fashion at various times, which could be applied to the internal walls in the Victorian and Edwardian periods, were picture rails at high level, just below the ceiling. Dado rails are positioned around waist height in entrance halls and perhaps also in any areas where a chair rail would be appropriate to avoid the wall decorations becoming damaged. Skirting boards have not been subject to fashion and consequently removed when they went out of fashion, as they serve a functional purpose of covering the junction between the base of the wall and where it joins the floor. The decorative details of skirting boards ranged from a simple rectangular section of timber on upper floors, to very ornate and decorative skirting boards in entrance halls and the main reception rooms. Functional rooms like sculleries tended not to have skirting boards in them, but a room with a hard floor may have had a rendered version to take the knocks. The range of wall finishes that were used depended on costs, so that more expensive finishes, such as wallpaper and tiled walls, were used to create an impression. Within the last few decades there have been changes in fashions between wall coverings like paper and plain paint, and this has been true further back in time.

This shows the rear face of a timber framed wall, where one side of a lath and plaster wall had inexplicably been removed, which is why there are white horizontal lines from the removed plaster on the diagonal timber and nail holes where the timber laths have been removed on the vertical timber studs.

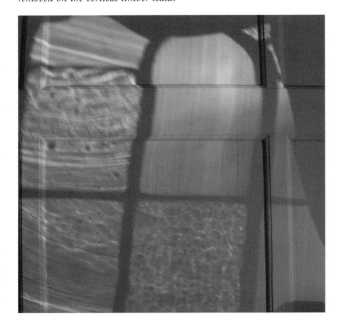

Timber panelling may be full height in a room or, as is often found in hallways of Edwardian houses, half-height panelling called dado panelling may be found.

To make a level surface to a timber framed wall. horizontal timber laths are fixed to vertical timber studs and then plaster is applied to the laths. This is a reverse view. The plaster is pushed through the gaps between the laths, so that it forms a hook over the top of the lath that is called a key. When the plaster dries, it keeps the plaster firmly in place. Where laths have inexplicably been removed, the impressions of the white horizontal lines of lime remain on the vertical timber posts, together with the nail holes.

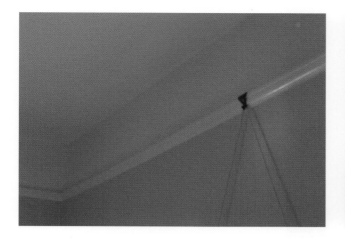

The white colour of the ceiling was brought down to the line of the picture rail to add interest to the room and perhaps increase the white area able to reflect light, and was a popular device in Victorian and Edwardian homes to reduce the apparent height of the ceiling. When lower ceilings were introduced after the Second World War, the use of a picture rail was no longer necessary to visually reduce the height of the ceiling.

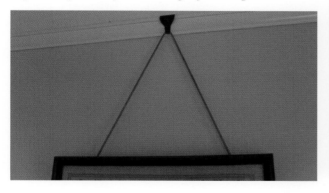

Picture rails are horizontal rails that are fixed around the walls of rooms at high level, so that pictures can be hung from the rails, using metal picture hooks. Picture rails were a popular method for hanging pictures, especially in houses that were rented, which was the majority up until the middle of the twentieth centaury. This was so that tenants could hang their own pictures on the walls and take them down when they moved, without damaging the walls. In addition, picture rails had a practical purpose, as where a house had lath and plaster walls, it was difficult to fix nails into the wall, so a picture rail meant that the pictures could be placed anywhere along the wall, rather than just where the vertical timber studs were in the underlying construction to which nails could be fixed.

The cut cross-section of the timber picture rail to the right shows how a picture rail clip was hung over this timber rail to allow pictures to be hung anywhere along this rail without damaging the wall.

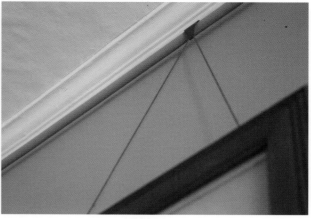

Brass picture rods were a popular way of hanging heavy pictures in the Georgian period, which could be hung on brass chains.

A metal picture hook was necessary to hook the picture over the timber picture rail.

Where an internal corner is created within a room, it is difficult to create a plaster corner that will not be vulnerable to damage, so a way of overcoming this is to create an architectural feature using a timber bead.

Dado rails are a timber rail that is placed around the wall at around the height of chair backs in halls, dining rooms and other public areas, where chair backs may be present that could damage the wall decoration. Dado rails tend to be of timber, but plaster rails are sometimes found. They were particularly popular in Victorian houses, but many were removed, when fashions changed, so a relatively small number of these now remain.

This dado rail is in the same room as the previous photograph, but is to a different design as one is a later addition or replacement than the other.

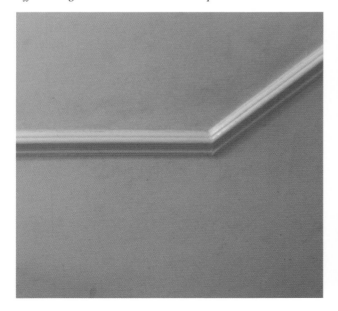

This is a typical Victorian dado design for an entrance hall that is used to keep the wall from being damaged and perhaps also served to keep dusty paint from flowing dresses.

This Victorian hallway shows how the dado rail and the skirting board are finished off at the base of the staircase.

Each Victorian and Edwardian staircase is detailed in slightly different ways and this has a continuous skirting rail by comparison with the previous picture.

Just below the change in direction of the dado rail, is a bend in the wall where the brick wall reduces in thickness.

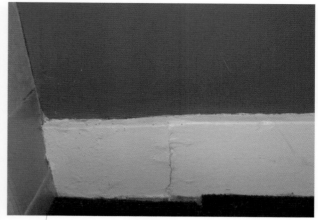

This is a plain, square-edged board that was used in rooms where decoration was not thought appropriate, such as attic rooms and kitchen areas.

This shows the detail of a 'torus' moulded skirting board, which was popular in the Victorian and Edwardian periods.

Skirting boards are a timber board that is applied over the junction between the wall and the floor, to make the joint look more attractive. They are also a protection against damage to the base of the wall. The height of the skirting board depended on the height and proportions of the room in which it was used. The detail on the top of the skirting board ranged from a square top to decorative mouldings, depending on the room or area in which the skirting board was located. A typical and popular type of skirting moulding in many Victorian and Edwardian houses was called a 'torus' moulding.

This is a Victorian example of a 'torus' skirting moulding that was the most common type of moulding detail for skirting boards.

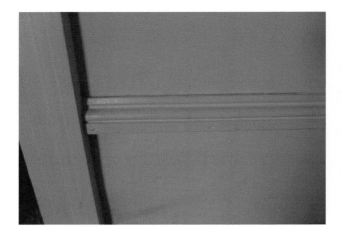

Sometimes a skirting detail could be little more than a moulding applied to a rendered base of the wall, as in this Edwardian example, where a smaller moulding was used to cover the junction of two types of wall finish.

The stair construction copies the skirting board moulding.

Wallpaper is often used to create a decorative effect on a wall. This method of decoration only became possible once large printing rollers were developed in the Victorian period. Later layers of wallpaper are often applied over older layers, when fashions changed. Embossed papers were also popular, as were flock wallpapers, which have a surface texture to them. This paper is possibly a later Victorian design and was found in the back of a cupboard, as it had not been redecorated when the rest of the room had been re-papered.

Embossed wallpapers were often used below the dado rail on staircases as they were more resilient to knocks and damage than other types of paper, when they became popular from around the end of the nineteenth century.

One layer of wallpaper was often applied over the previous layer, as in this case, and remains of earlier colour schemes may be found in places where the redecoration failed to obscure all traces of previous wallpapers.

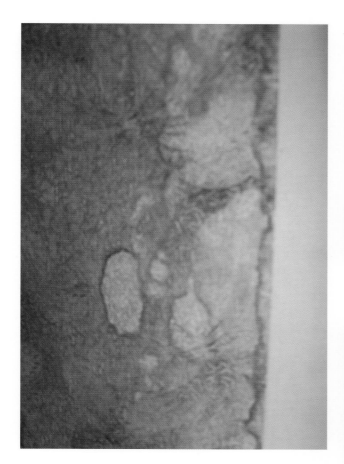

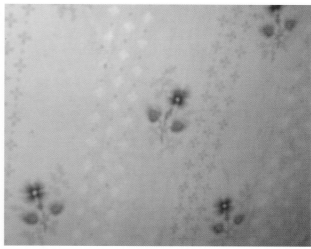

Wallpapers of all dates are a part of the history of the house and should be kept as a record of the history of the house.

This paper may date from the early part of the twentieth century, but it is still a part of the history of the house. Often rolls of wallpaper were used up in cupboards, so the paper may originally have been used in another part of the house.

Reproductions of older wallpaper designs are now available, and some wallpaper manufacturers are able to reproduce old wallpapers to suit a variety of tastes.

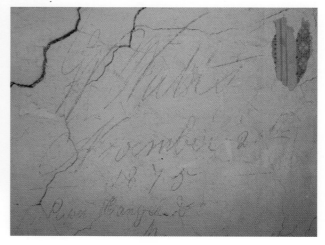

Embossed wallpapers were designed to be painted and underlying layers are still a record of how a house was painted in the past and should be preserved. Where a wall has emulsion paint on it, the paint may have been used to cover earlier wallpaper.

This scrap of wallpaper is datable as the decorators signed the wall in 1875.

Floors

The history of the type of floor finishes that were used in houses has developed not only with building technology, but also with the type of technology that was available to clean them. This has meant that the earliest types of flooring were those that could be swept clean, so brick, stone, tiles and timber boards were popular. Rugs could be laid over timber floors and they would periodically have to be lifted out to shake clean. It was only with the advent of the vacuum cleaner that fitted carpets could be laid in rooms, which completely obscured the floor surface. This development only became generally affordable during the middle part of the twentieth century.

The type of floor used in a particular room depended on its functional purpose. For example, areas where domestic work was carried out in a house, such as kitchens, usually had hardwearing surfaces that were easy to keep swept clean or mopped, while areas such as entrance halls and sitting rooms were designed to impress visitors. Patterned tiles were popular in Victorian entrance halls, while rugs were often laid in sitting rooms, so that the only area of timber boarding that would be seen was around the edges of the rugs. This meant that expensive timber finishes could be used just around the edges of rooms where they would be on display. Stone may also have been used in heavily-trafficked areas, particularly where the locally available building material was durable stone, which made it less expensive than using materials that would have had to be transported from further away.

Upper floors had little choice but to be built on a timber structure, and a timber finish was usually the first choice. Alternative structural floors include brick or stone vaulting, often found over cellars, which could then be finished with hard surface materials as if over the ground. Also there was a, now quite rare, material called a lime ash floor that could be used to span between timber floor joists and was broadly a compound based upon lime mortar and wood ash, which could be reinforced and bound together with sticks and straws to be self-supporting over the short spans between joists.

The joints between bricks may be quite narrow, so that there is no need for any mortar or sand to fill the joints; this is called dry jointing.

This is an example of a brick floor that has had considerable use over the years.

There are many patterns that a brick floor can be laid in and this is a typical design.

Brick floors were popular in areas where a hardwearing surface was required and were used mainly in kitchen and sculleries, often not being full depth bricks but special brick 'pavers'.

Sometimes two types of brick may be found, which can invite speculation about the house's history.

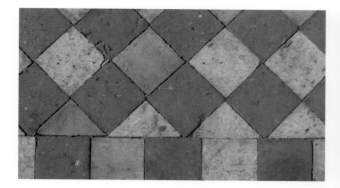

These are square terracotta tiles regionally called 'pamments', which are similar to square quarry tiles. The difference is that modern quarry tiles have a dense, hard surface, whereas traditional versions have a surface similar to the face of a brick. Both types of tiles were popular in cottages and farmhouses because of their robust and functional nature.

These Norfolk pamment tiles are laid in a square pattern.

Victorian quarry tiles were popular in areas of hard wear, such as sculleries.

This gives an idea of the Victorian designs that were popular. They were created using a small number of encaustic tiles that have a multi-coloured pattern within the tile, and single coloured tiles of different shapes that are combined to create intricate patterns.

In grander houses with vaulted brick or stone cellars it would be possible to have expensive marble floors laid on top rather than just timber.

This is a typical design for a tiled floor in an entrance hall to a Victorian house.

This design uses a combination of encaustic tiles and single colour tiles to create a different pattern.

These narrow floorboards indicate that they are Victorian, as floorboards decreased in width from the Georgian period through to the Victorian period. These floorboards are cut around the side of a marble hearth.

This floor uses single-colour tiles of differing sizes and shapes to create the pattern.

Where these Victorian floorboards have been stained around the edges of a room indicates where a rug has been laid in the centre of the room.

Timber was necessary for flooring on the upper floors and the age of a floor may be indicated by the width of the floorboards. These wide boards indicate that they are Georgian in origin. The earth and straw mixture under the boards was probably used as sound deadening between floors.

Most floorboards were not usually intended to be on display and so the timber from which the floorboards were cut was of a lower quality than would have been necessary if they were to be seen.

Repairs are often carried out on floors, so the pattern that is made where boards have been cut, may give a clue as to why the boards were cut in the first place.

This ceiling has been removed, at some time in the past, as the nail holes in the joists indicate where the timber laths were previously fixed. This has revealed the underside of the floorboards on the floor above and shows how they have been laid over the floor joists.

These Victorian floorboards have been inexpertly patched.

This is a typical design of parquet wood-block floor, laid in a herringbone pattern, which was generally used in entrance halls. Parquet flooring can take many forms but often is a hardwood or pine floor, made from about an inch-thick pieces of timber, which are laid in a layer of hot pitch tar to secure them in place. The individual pieces may have shaped sides to lock together.

Sometimes the ceriling of the room below is directly attached to the floorboards above.

The proportions of the individual pieces of timber may vary from floor to floor.

Chapter 7 Internal Doors and Window Features

Doors

Doors are necessary for privacy and help to keep the occupants of rooms warm in winter. Glazed doors allow people to see if other people are approaching the other side of the door and perhaps, more importantly, they are used to allow light, 'borrowed light', to illuminate otherwise gloomy areas. Obscured glass may be used so that areas are allowed to have light without loss of privacy. Panelled doors were a typical design for formal internal doors from the Georgian period into the twentieth century; thereafter, plywood allowed doors to be produced with larger panels, or even in one single piece. Within the design of a panel door there were numerous variations that were available, from the number of panels incorporated into the door, to whether there were mouldings around each panel and, if so, how ornate or simple they might be and whether the panel itself was recessed from the face of the door, or in the same plane as the frame around the door panels. The hierarchy of mouldings on doors was carefully thought through, as some doors may have mouldings on one side of a door and not on the other, depending on where the door is located within the house. Such rooms as cupboards or storeroom doors usually had no mouldings on the exterior to indicate the function of the room behind the door but equally, they may have had mouldings on the outside to match neighbouring doors but none inside, where no one could admire them. Vertically boarded doors were less expensive to make and tended to be used in more functional areas of the house, such as attics and under-stair cupboards. All doors would be fitted with ironmongery, the term used to describe the mainly metal (but also china and wood and, later, also plastic) components that are used on doors, such as hinges, door knobs and handles. Hinges are usually made of iron that generally gets painted. Where a door is intended to make an impression, then brass hinges (which need not be painted, even outside) are a more expensive and showy alternative. Door handles could be made of timber, iron, brass, bronze, various alloys and china. In the 1930s, a new type of (brown) plastic material called 'Bakelite' was developed and widely used for door knobs and handles. Some of the designs have survived to this day, manufactured in modern plastics. These early plastic features are sometimes used as replacement door knobs or handles on earlier doors when fashions changed and, though sometimes incongruous, they have now become a part of the history of the house. Where boarded doors were used, these tended to have latches used on them, which have a thumb pad at the top of the handle that is used as a pressure release for the latch on the other side of the door. Some of the earliest were made of timber, but most survivors are iron. Fingerplates were a popular Victorian idea, and they were used in areas where protecting the paintwork on doors was important, such as in rooms or hallways that visitors would see, so these

protective plates were placed near to the door handle. They would serve a, perhaps unintentional, additional purpose of isolating users from contact with the, toxic, lead paint used in the past. They could be made from timber, glass, brass or iron. The type of material used often depended on the architectural style of the room and the features of the door.

This is a typical four-panel Victorian door that has moulding around each of the panels.

This shows how a decorative moulding is used to cover the junction between the panels and the framing of the door.

This door has square-edged panels and is typical of doors used for service areas of the house.

This shows a panel door where the joint between the door and the panel is a square edge, which was cheaper to make than a door with mouldings. These types of doors were used for service rooms and often servants' quarters, as well as storerooms.

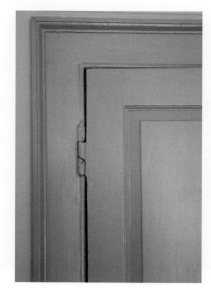

This shows a raised and fielded panel, which is where the panel is on the same plane as the surrounding framing of the door.

This is a popular design of architrave moulding, the classically-inspired 'ogee' that was used around the outside edge of the door frame, to cover the joint between the timber door frame and the adjoining wall's plaster. This moulding was a popular profile for architrave mouldings throughout the Victorian and Edwardian periods and has remained in production ever since.

Two-panelled doors became popular again at the end of the Victorian period and stayed in use during the 1920s and 1930s. They were popular because they were simpler to make than a four-panel door, as they had fewer components – even if skill was needed to butt join the planks necessary to make up the larger panels. Only after the Second World War in the 1940s did flush doors, which are doors without panels, become popular, as the techniques for manufacturing very large sheets of composite wood, such as plywood, were becoming more widespread. Where the wallpaper has been removed from the wall on the left side of this door, this has revealed where a dado rail has previously been removed – the outline of the dado rail is still visible. A dado rail formed a division that the Victorians found useful since they could place more durable decorative materials below the rail (such as painted, textured wall-coverings made from compressed paper or composites) and leave the upper areas in relatively fragile distempers and wallpaper.

This is a typical design of door from the 1930s, which was often adapted to have a glass upper panel.

Glazed Doors

The style of doors developed with progress in the size of the pieces of glass that could be produced. During the Georgian period, glass was made by blowing a large bubble of molten glass that was then spun into a disk. This method of making glass is called 'crown' glass and resulted in relatively small, and expensive, panes rarely much larger than a modern sheet of ordinary A4 paper. With the introduction of mechanized glass production in the Victorian period, which used mechanized rollers for glass-making, this enabled larger sheets of glass to be made. As this larger glass was heavier, the frames that supported it needed to be stouter. The increased use of glass in doors enabled darker spaces to be illuminated behind doors, in an era before electric lighting, while still retaining privacy by the use of obscured glass. During the Victorian and Edwardian periods, a large number of different designs of patterned and coloured glasses were used in doors. A typical design of internal glazed-door, during the Victorian period, was a door with nine panels of glass in it. These could either be of equal size or could be designed to have one larger panel in the middle and smaller panels around the edge, which provided the opportunity to use decorative patterns of etched and coloured glass in the corners.

This obscured patterned glass door has nine equal panels in the door.

Here is an example of a door that uses different colours of glass in the outer panels with nine panels of different sizes.

A typical Victorian design was to use red or blue glass corner panels in this type of door. In this case, the central panel has been replaced with a more recent, toughened glass.

This is a typical Victorian design for the glass in the corners of these doors.

Patterns and colours were popular in Victorian glass designs.

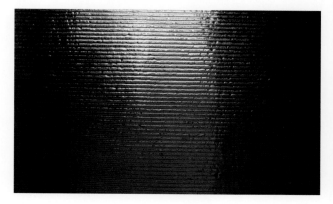

This Victorian glass with this pattern is often called reeded glass.

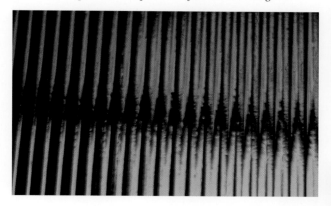

This reeded glass has wider reeds and suggests that it is later in date than the previous example.

There are various designs of obscured glass in this door: the middle panel is a popular patterned glass of the early twentieth century, while the bottom section is etched glass from Edwardian times with a cross motif.

These glazed doors have acid-etched glass in them that allows light into these dark areas while retaining privacy.

This Victorian glass has one face that is etched, so that it feels rough to the touch, while the other side of the glass has a smooth finish.

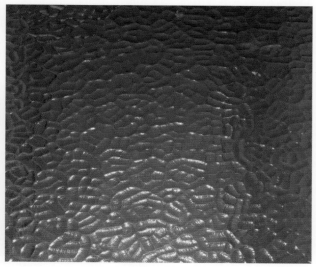

This is a popular design of patterned glass where the pattern is on one side, while the other face of the glass is smooth, which helps cleaning.

Borrowed Lights

This is the name used for an internal fanlight, which is the area above a door that is glazed. This feature allows light into an area, but still allows privacy to be retained within the room from which the light is 'borrowed'. These were a popular Victorian device and were used widely to ensure that light could illuminate otherwise dark areas.

A typical fanlight over a door gave a considerable amount of light into adjoining areas.

This corridor would be very dark without the use of borrowed lights from the adjoining rooms.

Boarded Doors

In medieval houses, doors tended to be boarded, but with the arrival of the Georgian period, panelled doors became much more fashionable, so that these 'old-fashioned' boarded doors tended to be used now in areas such as storerooms or areas that were generally out of the way or less used, as these tended to be cheaper to construct. The bracing of the door tended to be on the side of the door that was less important. These doors tended to be used with strap hinges, which were mounted on the face of the door, as concealed hinges were not suited to this type of door because of their construction, as there was no frame at the edge to fix to. They often had a patch lock on one side of the door or a latch to operate them. As there was only the thickness of the boarding over most of the door, there was no space into which to recess a concealed 'mortice' latch.

This shows the front face of a boarded door in a Victorian cellar.

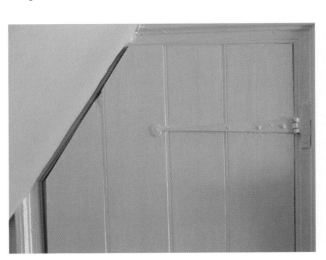

Boarded doors tended to be used for attic and cellar rooms, as they were cheaper to make than four-panelled doors. It was also easier to cut them to fit the size of the door opening.

This shows the back of a typical boarded door, again in a cellar area.

Ironmongery

Ironmongery (sometimes the more decorative elements are also called 'door furniture') is the term that includes hinges, door knobs and locks that are fixed to a door. They also help to indicate the original intended function and status of the door, along with the architectural styling of the door. Iron was popular on more functional doors. The word 'ironmongery' is a reminder of mediaeval practicality, while brass naturally became popular on doors that would be seen by visitors, and was more costly. The type of decorative details included decorative reeded handles, although timber, china and, later, Bakelite plastic, from the interwar years onwards, were also popular types of door knobs, according to their location within the house. Traditionally, door knobs were popular during the Victorian period, as these were paired with fairly large 'patch', surface-mounted locks and concealed 'mortice' locks, which allowed plenty of room to grasp the handle without knocking knuckles on the door frame. Only with the later use of more compact mortice locks fitted within the door, did lever handles become necessary and popular, since they allowed the hand operating them to be kept clear of the door edge. Lever handles were also promoted by a change in fashion at the end of the Victorian period, as designers used them extensively in Arts and Crafts style houses.

Door knobs were of many shapes and designs, depending on the door.

This china door knob also has a smaller china handle that is used for the door lock.

This is a typical example of a brass door-knob that has a reeded pattern to it for additional grip. It is matched by the adjoining keyhole cover plate, called an escutcheon plate.

This door knob is made of ebony.

This is typical surface-mounted lock and brass knob.

This is a typical blacksmith's iron latch that has a bolt below the handle, and its mechanism is visible.

This is an example of a Bakelite-style plastic door knob, which must have been a replacement during the 1930s, as the lock and door dates from the Victorian period.

Door knobs are often replaced or re-used on different doors, so finding older examples still in use is rare.

This Edwardian lock has a more decorative back plate and a reeded door knob.

This is a lever handle made from an early plastic from the 1930s called Bakelite. Although these are usually replacements on Victorian and Edwardian houses, they are also a part of the historical development of the house.

This shows how a door latch works on both sides.

The design of Victorian door latch had decorative elements incorporated into them.

This is a hand-made door latch with thumb latch dating from the Georgian period.

Finger plates were used to protect the door above and below the door knob, and were made from timber, glass, brass or Bakelite plastic. They were popular in the Victorian period and were often removed when they went out of fashion later on. Where a door has had fingerplates removed, the impression of it may still be visible on the door.

Decorative door-handles, like this Victorian example, may often be removed when a door is being repainted and replaced, but as they are a part of the history of the house, they should be retained for future interest.

This door chain has a decorative design on the end of the chain.

Security bolts were usually mounted on the face of the door.

This design of door hinge is a development from the previous H-shaped, face-mounted hinge that dates from the Georgian period or earlier. The design of the hinge shows that the timber joints in the door frame were not thought to be that strong. The door panel can also be seen to be roughly bevelled here in order to fit into the frame, so this is a very basic version of a raised fielded door.

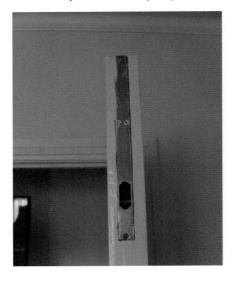

Recessed bolts, like this, are used to keep one of a pair of doors in place, where the bolts need to be more discrete.

This is a 'parliament hinge' that allows the door to be opened flat against the wall without hitting the door frame's projecting architrave moulding.

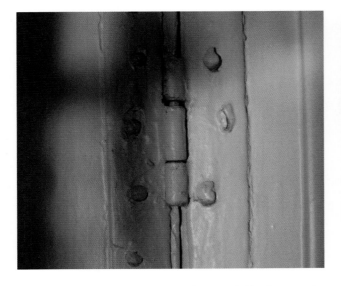

Early hinges were face fixed on doors and were probably often re-used.

This shows a parliament hinge when the door is opened against the wall.

Window Features

The internal features on windows are to enable them to be opened and closed more easily and to keep the windows fixed shut. As with door 'furniture' and ironmongery, the fittings on windows would be available in both basic and highly decorated versions. The security features on the windows themselves are usually made of metal, such as brass or iron, while the decorative features that surround window frames may range from timber mouldings to plaster decoration. The type of glazing bar holding the glass usually gives an indication of the date of the window, as thin glazing bars were popular during the Georgian period, and would be suitable for thin and lightweight Georgian glass, becoming thicker during the Victorian period to cope with larger sheets of thicker, heavier glass, until intermediate glazing bars could be made redundant when larger sheets of glass were able to be manufactured.

There were several types of sash fasteners that grip the sashes together to secure them; one slides into the catch plate (top), *while the other has a turn screw* (bottom).

Where the glass meets the timber on a sash window, there is usually a decorative moulding. A traditional type of moulding was called 'lamb's tongue'.

This type of sash fastener works by squeezing the sashes together.

The joint between the window frame and the surrounding wall may have a timber moulding placed over it or a decorative design applied, using a putty-like substance, called gesso, that was used for repetitive patterns; it is relatively soft and can be easily damaged.

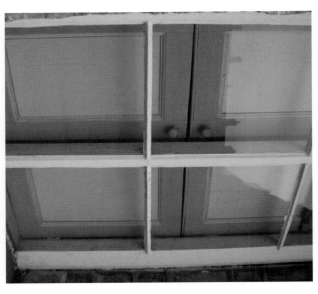

This is a typical design for a casement window fastener called a 'monkey tail'.

These shutters will evidently be on display in the room on the wall adjacent to the window, like a pair of doors, when they are opened.

Internal shutters were popular in the Georgian and Victorian periods for security, as well as keeping the heat within a room. Usually shutters are hung on hinges from the side of the windows and may be concealed inside boxes either side of the window during the day. This is a more unusual example, where vertical sliding shutters, hung on sash cords like a second pair of windows, drop down into a slot under the window during the day. Other examples still exist of shutters that slid sideways on tracks into a concealed cavity within the wall thickness.

This is an example of obscured Victorian glass.

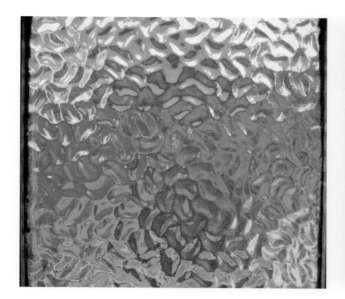

This is another type of patterned glass that was popular in the Victorian and Edwardian periods.

This pattern of glass allows light in without compromising the privacy of the room behind. It was very popular in the mid-twentieth century.

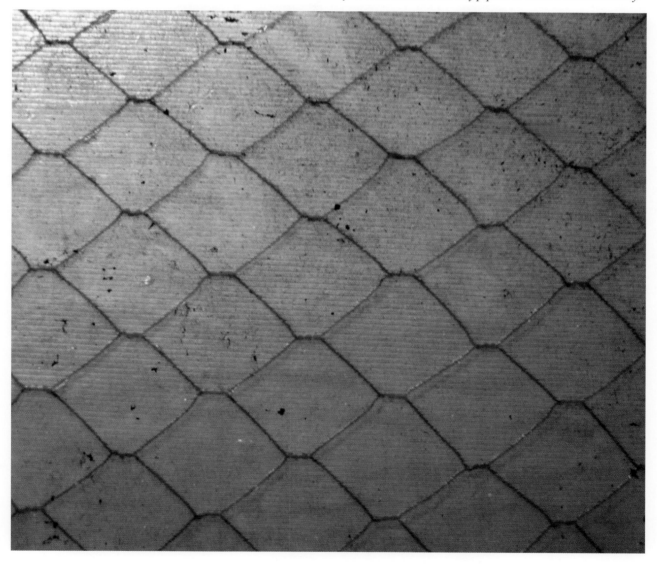

Casting glass around a wire mesh was found to improve security and fire resistance and this technique was refined during the twentieth century until eventually superseded by modern laminated glass, which incorporates a sheet of translucent plastic instead.

Chapter 8 Architectural Features – Staircases, Fireplaces and Details

Staircases

Staircases are often the first feature that is seen when entering a house. For this reason they tended to be embellished to indicate the status of the house. The most impressive part of a staircase is usually the newel post at the start of the staircase, which is used to secure the handrail in place at the bottom of the stair. The balusters are the slender vertical posts that join the stair tread to the handrail and, in addition, they are used to prevent anyone or anything from falling from the stairs or at least to indicate the danger. The design of balusters developed from slender square posts, which were popular in Georgian houses, to ornately turned, circular, timber balusters in the Victorian period, which may have been inspired by mediaeval and classical traditions. With the arrival of the Arts and Crafts period at the end of the nineteenth century, wider timber slats, which may have had decorations cut into them, were preferred to 'turned' balusters as a change in fashion. The design and complexity of the balustrades on upper floors and to the basement was often to a simpler design, as these areas were not expected to be seen by anyone who did not live or work in the house. There were two designs for how the balusters were jointed to the steps: either they were stepped up from each step or they were in a continuous line of even-length balusters that rose from a 'string', the long side-member of the stair. Handrails tended to be made from hardwoods, so that they were not painted and, apart from being a practical way to avoid the wear of a painted rail, this may also have served to avoid hand contact with the toxic lead paint of the period. The material that the staircase is made from was also indicative of the status of the house, so that grand houses may have had stone used from the main floors to the upper floors, as well as to the basements sometimes; the latter probably for more practical reasons of wear-resistance than show. However, the majority of houses had timber staircases, which could be covered according to preference with a stair carpet over the central part of the stairs, called a stair runner.

An impressive newel-post is used at the base of the staircase, and the balusters are stepped in line with the steps in this Victorian house.

This is a design for a Victorian open-ended stair tread.

This is a Victorian example of where the steps are enclosed at the side by a 'string', which both enables the stairs to be constructed spanning the space, like a ladder, and also allows the balusters to be spaced more economically and to be of equal length and design.

The designs of newel posts were many and varied in the Victorian period; this newel post has been made by turning it on a lathe and the top of the newel post has been shaped into an acorn.

This staircase has the balusters of equal length and fixed to a string that covers the ends of the steps in this Victorian house.

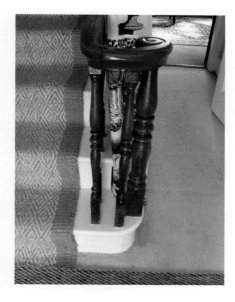

This is a design of newel post that has a curved handrail; making such handrails was a fine art in itself and involved secretly joining separately carved pieces of timber together.

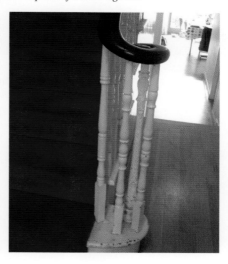

This curved handrail has a cast-iron column in the background to anchor the stair in place.

This is a Gothic-inspired example of a Victorian newel-post.

Stone stairs were often used to the basement to allow for the heavy traffic between the ground and basement floors. The metal handrail is indicative of the status of the stair. Sometimes stone staircases may have been painted later in their history.

This is an example of a typical single-flight Victorian staircase.

Straight stairs were typical in Victorian houses, as the width of Victorian building plots was usually narrower than those for Edwardian houses, which may have allowed space for a turn in the staircase.

Stairs that may have been used only by domestic servants tended to be of a much simpler design than the main staircase to the house.

The turn of a staircase on a staggered landing allowed the handrail to be continuous.

Details like these turned pendants at the base of upper newel-posts are typical of the design details used on a Victorian staircase.

There are subtle indicators on a staircase like this where change from ornate balusters to a more simple design indicates that the rooms on the upper floors were not intended to receive visitors.

The steps at the corner are called 'winders' and the skirting board is carved around these steps, which are cut into the board to secure the steps in place.

A timber staircase is constructed on timbers that run the length of the stair, and the treads and risers are kept tightly together with blocks and wedges to try to limit creaking.

Fireplaces

These are usually the most impressive, as well as functional, feature in a room. In addition, they were, for many centuries, the sole source of heating a room, before central heating began to become affordable for the majority of homeowners, from the 1960s onwards. Right up to that time, purchasers of a new house spent as much, if not more, time selecting a fireplace than kitchen or bathroom fittings. The materials that were used to make the decorative fire surrounds ranged from marble, slate and other stones to cast iron and timber. As the designs of fire surrounds in the main living areas were a way for the architectural significance of a room to be expressed, fire surrounds may have been one of the first items to be altered within a house, when a house changed ownership. Fireplaces were more likely to be updated or replaced in previous generations, in the same way that kitchens and bathrooms are now altered and updated by modern owners, as fashions change.

Marble Fire-Surrounds

Marble fire-surrounds were popular in Victorian and Edwardian houses. The convention was that white marble was used in drawing rooms and the more feminine rooms, while black was used in dining rooms and studies, and rooms set aside for male activities. The shape and style of fire surrounds depended on the size of the room and the architectural style.

Victorian marble fire-surrounds were designed around the fire grate, which, in this example, is an arch-headed fire grate.

Where the fire grate included a tiled splay, the surround was designed accordingly.

Georgian fire-surrounds favoured roundels in the corners.

This Georgian marble fire-surround has been closed off, but luckily not removed, when central heating was installed in the 1930s.

This fire surround has brackets supporting the mantle shelf.

Black fire-surrounds were generally used in dining rooms, so where the function of a room has changed over time, the colour of the marble for the fire surround may give an indication of the former use of the room.

This nineteenth-century marble fire-surround has had a 1930s coal fire inserted into it, as the beige-coloured tiles were typical of this period. The colour of the fire surround indicates that this was formerly used as a dining room during the Victorian period.

Stone Fire-Surrounds

These were popular in stone areas but also imported into other areas, while intricately carved ones that mimicked castle features were used for Gothic-revival houses in the late-nineteenth century.

Slate Fire-Surrounds

Slate was a popular material used for fire surrounds, which may have been embellished with a finish in order to give it an impression of being marble – a more expensive material.

Scraping away at the paint in an inconspicuous area should reveal the original material and finish of a fireplace that has been painted.

Finding a fire surround that has not been painted over during the twentieth century is a rare find, as these were often painted when fashions wanted to break from the past and give rooms a lighter feel. Of course sometimes they were removed completely.

Timber Fire-Surrounds
Timber fire-surrounds were popular in all types of rooms, as they could be decoratively designed for formal areas with ornate and decorative carving, or they could be simply designed for bedrooms and attics where simpler designs were appropriate. While timber may have not been so popular for Victorian reception rooms, the use of timber came back into popularity during the Arts and Crafts period at the end of the century, as a reaction to marble and slate fireplaces that were popular during the Victorian period. Where public rooms in houses had impressive materials or decoration used on the fire surrounds, bedrooms, attics and servants' rooms may have had more simply detailed fire-surrounds that were often made of timber.

A simple, timber fireplace that has been subtly embellished with ordinary joinery mouldings.

A delicate timber fire-surround with gesso mouldings applied to it enabled householders to afford the appearance of a luxuriously carved classical-style fireplace.

After the popularity of slate and marble for fire surrounds during the Victorian period, there was a return to timber fire-surrounds during the Arts and Crafts period at the end of the nineteenth century.

A fire surround can be as simple as a square timber-frame with a shelf on top. This design was typical in bedrooms and attic rooms in Victorian houses. The central part of the fire surround is made of cast iron with an arch-headed grate, which was a universally popular design during the Victorian period.

Cast-Iron Fire-Surrounds

Once the technique of producing cast iron had been established, and there were trains to move them around the country, then iron fire-surrounds became more popular for use in Victorian and Edwardian houses. While cast iron had long been used for the inner part of the fire surround where the coal burned, complete all-in-one cast-iron fire-surrounds were a logical development. The decorative details and size of cast-iron fire-surrounds could be quite ornate or plain, depending on where the surround was to be located, whether it was in a sitting room or in a bedroom.

This cast-iron fire-surround has not been painted.

The detail in a cast-iron fire-surround can be quite decorative, but many years of paint applied to such fire surrounds, may obscure much of the detail.

Some iron fire-surrounds were intended to look metallic, like the iron cooking ranges that preceded them, but others would be comfortable with a painted finish.

Tiled Fire-Grates and Surrounds

Two types of fire surrounds had tiles inserted in them. All-in-one surrounds had tiles in the cheeks, while the inserts for other surrounds could also have tiles added into them.

The tiles and cheeks of a fire surround were often matched to each other so that, if they look very different, it may be that one or other element was changed for some reason.

Tiles in the cheeks of fireplaces could either be plain or decorative.

The splayed tiles reflected more heat out into the room.

In the 1930s and 1940s, tiled fireplaces like this were popular, echoing the Art Deco and other exotic influences that were a break with the past.

The semicircular plate at the back of this grate is opened to get the fire going and then may be regulated to reduce the airflow over the coals or shut completely when there is no fire.

The size of grate for use with coal was smaller than those used with wood, as the logs needed a larger basket to hold them while they were burned.

This cast-iron fire-grate, has pivots on the front for trivets that would be used to swing platforms into the fire, which had a kettle placed on them, so they were used to heat the water, and used for, in effect, dual purposes.

This is a proprietary type of coal grate designed with various built-in features to make the burning of coal more economical, hence it was marketed as a Parson's grate.

Hearths

Hearths can be made from any non-combustible material, such as stone, slate or, later on, tiles were used.

The purpose of the hearth is to protect floor surfaces from around the fire from being damaged by burnt embers falling out of the fire on to the floor. This hearth is of stone, but many types of inert material were used. Traditionally, a hearth would nearly always be accompanied by a fender made of metal or wood covered with metal, whose purpose was to keep burning embers from rolling off the fire onto wooden floors and rugs, and to a certain extent to keep people back from danger.

Tiles in a range of colours were used for hearths and the relief tiles for the splayed surround on the fire surround.

Architectural Features

There are many features that may still be found in houses that contribute to the architecture of the rooms.

Wall Features

Walls tend generally to be plastered and, therefore, form a background surface on which other features may be applied. The style and type of feature depend on the use of the room and its hierarchy within the house.

Embossed wallpaper used to give definition to a dado panel in a hallway.

Timber-Framed Features and Access Hatches
There are many details in a house that may be made of timber and to enhance an otherwise functional part of the house; these details can be turned into architectural features.

A roof access hatch still has a decorative element with a bead moulding to the edge of each plank.

The access hatch to this roof space is a framed door, with an architrave around the edges of the door.

This timber wall is made of bead moulding and makes an architectural feature of this otherwise functional wall, which divides the hall from the cellar area.

Even this panel to the side of a handrail has a decorative detail used around the edges that lifts it out of plainness but it is arguably still expressing the necessary construction underneath.

Built-In Cupboards

Built-in cupboards are often taken out, to increase the space within a room. However, where they still exist, they form a part of the house and should be retained.

The interior face of cupboards may reveal earlier finishes, as with this door that was painted later in white paint, but this has flaked off to reveal a grained varnish finish that was popular from the Victorian times onwards.

There is a real art to carrying out paint effects such as dragging and graining successfully.

Alcoves and Arches

The areas between a fireplace and a wall are ideal for fitting movable pieces of furniture in them.

Decorative details, such as this arch, create an interesting additional feature to this room.

Much Victorian and Edwardian furniture was designed to fit the dimensions of the houses of the day, which is why this furniture fits so well into alcoves like this and is of the right height for the ceilings of the time.

Archways are a popular way of adding architectural details to walls. In this case, as a way of accommodating extra thickness in a wall where it was needed and reducing the cost of unnecessary bricks where it was not.

Bells and Bell Pushes

Many older houses may have remnants of older ways of life in them. One, in particular, is where houses reveal evidence of having had servants, which, until the social upheaval following the two World Wars, may have been found in more general housing stock, rather than just the very largest houses.

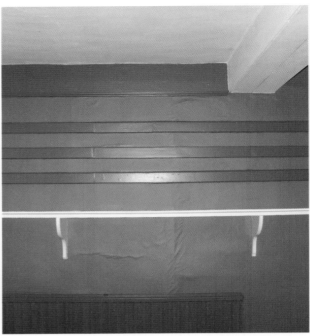

These servants' bells have probably been re-used in this location for the front door-bell, but remnants of the metal corner fixings may often be found in out-of-the-way places, where these have not been removed during later redecorations.

Boards found at high level may indicate where servants' bells were once located.

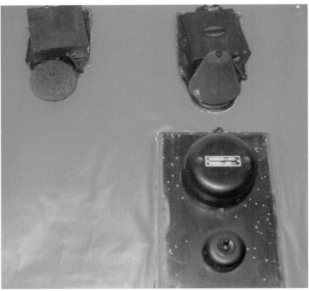

Bells to call servants were even made in Bakelite, showing that, in some houses, domestic service was still a way of life in the plastic age.

The type of electric bells that superseded the old, mechanical, pulley system.

Coat Hooks

Many halls had coat hooks, and very few of these remain, but where they do, they should be retained, for like other domestic ironwork, there is a chance that they are the products of a long-gone local foundry.

This gives an idea of how a row of hooks looked in a Victorian hall.

Victorian coat and hat hooks like these are unusual to find in a house, as many have been replaced over the years as fashions changed.

Historical Information

Often pieces of information come to light when decorating rooms.

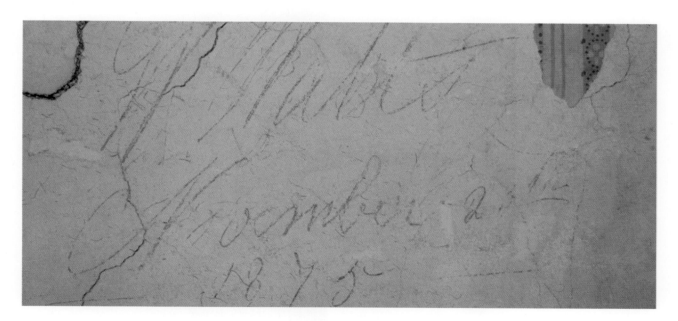

Historical clues are likely to be found in any house, such as this example where not only is the date of the work identified, but there is also a remnant of wallpaper that may precede this date on the wall.

Chapter 9 Functional Rooms – Kitchens, Bathrooms and Services

There are a number of rooms within a house that are functional rooms that were not designed for architectural show. Even so they may still retain fixtures and fittings that may be original to the house. Where these exist they should be retained for future generations to appreciate, as they are a part of the history of the house and its passage through time. Where these fittings survive, retaining them is important because so many have been removed from houses over the years, which makes those that are left comparatively rare. In previous generations, many fixtures and fittings remained intact, because these were functional areas of the house, rather than those that visitors would see, so there was little reason for them to be altered for fashionable reasons. However, other areas of the house, like the reception rooms, were more likely to be altered or changed as a result of fashions because these were the only areas that visitors would see. More recently, attentions have turned to kitchens and bathrooms as areas where alterations are likely to be carried out, as more visitors are likely to see these rooms than in previous periods during the history of the house. Where previous generations of house owners may not have seen any reason to make, say, a kitchen fashionable if it was rarely to be seen, the modern owner, who spends more time in the kitchen, needs to be aware of the history that surrounds them and this can sometimes mean having to exercise restraint to avoid sweeping interesting evidence of the past away in the name of a new passing fashion.

Kitchen Fittings

The idea of a modern kitchen is a recent development from the Victorian format of separating out the functions of a scullery, which was where the sink was located, and the kitchen, where preparation and cooking were carried out. The early scullery area did not necessarily have running water, but could have been supplied by a stand pipe or a pump or even a well. The scullery was the area where food was washed and dishes cleaned. The kitchen was where the cooking range was located; it had a double function of heating the room, as well as being the cooking facility. There would also be a separate storage area for food in a pantry, often a windowless room on a north-facing outside wall with plenty of air vents, as this was an age before the widespread adoption of the domestic refrigerator. The kitchen was a functional room rather than the extension of the living area that it has become in the present day. Because so many developments have happened in kitchens, from the arrival of electricity – which led to the development of new kitchen appliances – to the use of fitted kitchens, this has meant that it is rare to find many original kitchen fittings still remaining, as most have usually been

replaced, possibly several times over in the recent past. There may be small items leftover from a former era, such as shelves or ceiling hooks that have not been removed in various refurbishments. There may also be items of fixed furniture or areas like pantries with their stone cold-shelves, but usually most items have been removed or replaced, such as cooking ranges, which are no longer suitable for modern-day expectations. Sometimes remnants of white tiles are found at the back of cupboards, near where sinks may have previously been located. Tiles were often left in place, as they were often difficult to remove easily, and remained where they would not be visible and covered over, so they are able to give us valuable clues about the history of the house.

A kitchen table was an important part of a kitchen, and the floor tended to be solid, so that it could easily be washed down. This is why these glass cups became popular to keep the legs of furniture away from the water as otherwise they may have started to rot.

Dressers were a typical feature in kitchens where the crockery was kept ready for use.

218

The details on even functional furniture give an idea of the previous elegance that was attached to simple items.

Dressers were a popular feature of a kitchen and a sloping grove in any piece of furniture, like this, may indicate where plates were propped up in an upright position.

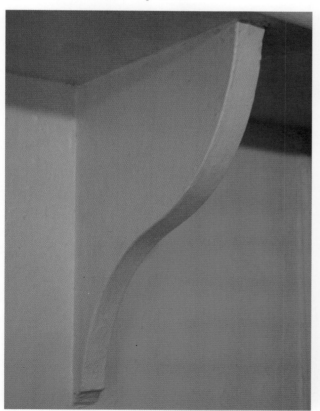

This shelf is a remnant of an earlier kitchen where open shelving was popular. Often older kitchen shelving and cupboards, when they have been removed, are used in storerooms or garages, for additional storage space.

The cooking range would have been located within a fireplace at the rear of a Victorian house. However, more recently, kitchens have been moved into the adjoining scullery and the previous kitchen has been made into a living area.

Bathroom Fittings

The introduction of bathrooms into houses was made possible at the end of the Victorian period, with the development of the sewer network and the introduction of piped running water and internal plumbing in houses. Originally, when there was no running water, washing happened with a jug and bowl, and there may have been a portable 'tin' bath filled with water heated on the kitchen range. Drains and running water allowed houses to adopt the water closet, as a development from the earth closet that was located away from the house. A privy would have either adjoined the outside of the house or was somewhere in the back garden. So the first WCs were attached to the house, still as outside features, but they had to be near to where the piped water supply and drains served the kitchen or scullery. Bathrooms that included a bath and washhand basin were added at a later date. In Victorian houses, usually the smallest bedroom was sacrificed to create a bathroom on the first floor. The other option was to locate it beyond the kitchen in the storerooms at the end of the ground floor. This means that bathroom fittings are a fairly recent introduction by comparison with the age of older houses. This also meant that plumbing pipes and waste pipes had to be introduced into an existing house in order for these elements to function. Older bathroom fittings are fairly rare and many have been replaced over the years. The earliest baths were usually cast iron with a glazed enamel finish and of a more or less standard, free-standing design. All baths, basins and WCs were usually white, although decorations may have been applied. It was only in the mid-twentieth century that coloured bathroom suites became fashionable. Water closets originally had high-level water cisterns, but in the 1960s, low-level toilet cisterns that were connected to the toilet pan became a popular feature. The traditional type of tap fitting used on all types of baths and basins was the cross-head tap.

This is a typical design of cast-iron roll-top bath with chrome cross-head taps and claw feet that was popular as the first design of bath fitted into a new bathroom, which was usually created from an existing bedroom.

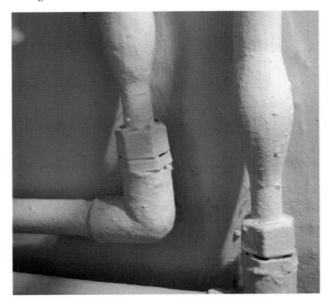

Original early twentieth century lead joints.

High-level toilet cisterns were used to increase the flow of water into the toilet pan.

White, glass splash-backs, like this, are contemporary with the date of the basin.

Modern high-level toilet cisterns are still available, although plastic cisterns have become a popular, cheaper choice. Modern low-level cisterns only became popular from the mid-twentieth century.

This is a typical design of chrome cross-head tap that was used for baths and basins, which often had the manufacturer's name on the white ceramic plate in the middle of the tap.

Where toilet cisterns have been replaced, the original lead pipe may have been retained, as in this case.

Early toilet seats developed from the garden privy's plank with a hole in. This is a replica of a typical design from the Edwardian period.

This cast-iron bracket is a popular design that was used to support high-level toilet cisterns. This bracket has since been re-used as a shelf bracket.

The small separate buildings in these gardens are a row of privies, which were used until the arrival of internal bathrooms.

The end lean-to building was probably the outside toilet before internal plumbing was adopted.

The glazed pantiles in the roof may indicate that this was a privy, which was sited away from the house. Often yew trees may be found near privies, as they were thought to have a cleansing effect on the area.

Here is another example of the outside toilet – behind the small, high window and added to the end of the original kitchen extension.

This may also be another example of a privy in the garden.

Re-Used Fittings

An old bath or a stone sink may have been put to some other purpose within the garden.

Where a house does not have the original fittings still present in the house, take a look around the garden, as old bathroom fittings were difficult to completely dispose of until the arrival of skips.

Old, stone sinks from the scullery may have been re-used as a planter. When square, white, china Belfast sinks were removed from kitchens, during the 1960s and 1970s, they were often disguised for use in gardens by being covered with a layer of mortar to conceal their white colour.

Services

This term usually covers water, gas and electricity, which are the utilities that flow in and out of the house and its surroundings, in order for it to function properly. The way in which these new services are integrated within the fabric of an existing house is a sensitive balancing act. Georgian houses had very little in the way of any of the modern services. Water was only available from wells and piped running water, as we know it today, did not exist. The Victorians initiated piped running water in towns but it was more than half-way through the twentieth century before the majority of rural areas could be said to have this facility. Modern-style kitchens and bathrooms followed in the wake of this service and the equally important mains sewerage services (although country areas are often still without mains sewers). Electricity supplies were still in their infancy at the beginning of the twentieth century, and it was not until much later that many rural dwellings had electricity or running water. Even today there are many rural properties that do not have gas supplies, so that they have to rely on oil or electricity for heating.

Because many houses were built before modern-day services were available, these services have had to be integrated into the fabric of the existing houses. This is often difficult to do sensitively and a great deal of care and initial thought has to be put into planning the introduction of these services, so that the final result is sympathetic and appropriate to the fabric of the existing house. Many early plumbing installations are made of lead pipes; as these were individually made by hand, there is often great artistry in these hand-crafted pieces of work. Many have since been replaced with standardized plastic fittings.

Prior to the introduction of running water, pumps like this were used to draw water up from wells. Unfortunately, this is one that has been removed from its original location.

This cast-iron soil stack has a decorated lead bracket used to fix it to the wall.

This top of a stench pipe, which takes foul smells away from the drains of a house, shows the workmanship that can be put into leadwork.

Even the large-diameter soil pipes from a house in cast iron can be rather elegant in themselves.

Lighting

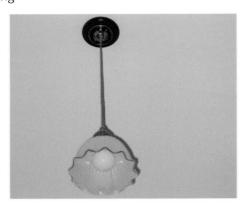

As lighting tends to be a later introduction into houses built before the Edwardian period, where any early light-fittings survive, they are likely to be later introductions or to have been converted from the positions that used gas or candles. The wiring that is used in a house will most likely have been replaced over the years, although remnants of early rubber and lead-covered cables may still be discovered in out-of-the-way places and in disused conduits – the outer casing, through which some wiring cables are threaded.

Simple but decorative glass and china fittings were the earliest form of lamp shades, unfortunately not matched in elegance by some modern energy-efficient bulbs.

This simple lamp shade is typical of early fittings, as used extensively in functional areas of the house, like kitchens and service areas.

This is another simple, early design of lamp shade that directly illuminates the area below.

As most Victorian houses were designed and built before the arrival of electricity, the houses were designed to ensure that they made the most of any naturally available light.

This is a typical design of glass shade from the early years of popular electric lighting.

Early twentieth century metal domed light switch.

In some houses there may be clues as to earlier forms of lighting, such as this stalk from a gas lamp pipe. The fitting has long gone, but the stalk is a useful historical guide.

Early wall socket.

Early light switches, such as this Bakelite switch, could be retained with the property, even if they are not usable, as they are a historical record of what would have been there.

Sometimes electric bell pushes, as this one made of Bakelite plastic from the 1940s, still remain in a house.

Heating

Heating systems in older houses started to be introduced at the end of the nineteenth century to public buildings and larger houses, but, generally, central heating did not become more universal until the 1960s and the advent of automatic gas and oil boilers or electric storage-heaters. The older style of heating systems relied on a single cast-iron water-circulation pipe in the 1920s, which passed the hot water through all the radiators in succession, propelled by 'gravity' or the tendency for hot water to rise above cooler water, so that a flow could be set up without any pump to return the cooled water back to the boiler, if the pipework were balanced correctly. The next development in central heating was a two-pipe system, which meant that after water had been through a radiator, it was then returned to the boiler in the return pipe to be heated up again for redistribution. This meant that the last radiator on the system received hot water, rather than luke-warm water, as it did not have to go through a lot of previous radiators, which would have reduced its level of heat. These systems changed to smaller diameter copper pipework after electric pumps were available to ensure an efficient and quick circulation. The style of radiators is a good indication of the date of a heating system within a house. Originally, radiators were made from cast iron, and column radiators and flat panels were typical designs, but later additions to the system, which date from the 1960s onwards, are likely to be of pressed, mild steel. These were single radiators to begin with but, double-thickness, pressed-panel radiators, were used from the 1980s onwards. The type of pipes used on the system is also indicative of the age of the heating system. Cast-iron pipes were used up until the 1960s, by which time smaller diameter copper pipes had been adopted for the pumped systems.

This shows the width of a typical low-height, column radiator.

This is a traditional type of radiator valve.

This is a typical design of column radiator from the early twentieth century.

This is a design of lower, wider, column radiator dating from the 1930s.

Flat-panel cast-iron radiators could be extended by adding additional panels to make a radiator larger.

1930s iron heating pipes.

Interestingly, this flat-panel radiator, dating from the 1940s, has been placed in front of the earlier form of heating, the open fire, which in this case is a Georgian marble fire-surround.

Parts of the original hot water installations may still survive.

This is a 1960s pressed-steel radiator.

This is a 1960s pressed-panel radiator that has had a towel rail added to it.

External Lighting
Before the arrival of electricity, external lighting was high maintenance, as each light had to be lit each night and the wicks of the lamps had to be trimmed. So, lamps were cleverly designed to offer as much light as possible from a single source. Some can be found that light both sides of a front door by being placed across a fanlight.

Lamps were hung away from the wall to give maximum illumination.

This is an example of a lamp over an entrance door.

This lamp is located between the two entrances to this house.

Part III: Sustainability and Energy Conservation

Preparing for the winter in the future may mean a return to gathering and storing wood, particularly in old houses, many of which were originally designed to burn this potentially carbon-neutral fuel.

Chapter 10 Sustainability and Energy Conservation

Living in an older house is sustainable in itself, as new resources have not been used up to construct a new house. The current area of focus is to reduce the amount of energy that is consumed within a house, now that more energy-consuming appliances have been introduced into houses, by comparison with those that were available in pervious centuries. In addition, we have grown to expect greater levels of comfort and warmth than previous generations, so that, while previous generations would consider ice on the inside of windows to be a normal part of living in a house, this is now not considered to be acceptable. Also, our predecessors wore more clothing and kept warm as a result of having to carry out many more manual tasks, for which we now have labour-saving devices to do these things for us. There may also have been a greater awareness of how to keep an existing house as warm as possible. For example, curtains or shutters were closed at night as a matter of course during the winter, as there was an understanding about how to keep the heat retained within a room of an evening to keep warm. The idea of occupants all being in the same room in a house, so that they all kept warm together, was a familiar concept. These habits have changed since the arrival of central heating has allowed people to spend time in different rooms that are all heated to the same temperature. Before the arrival of electric lighting during the twentieth century, evenings were spent by candle or oil-lamp light, and people tended to sit in one room to share the light; they tended to go to bed earlier, which also saved energy. Currently we are looking to reduce our fuel consumption in tandem with creating more of our own power domestically, rather than relying on supplies from further away.

Heat-Loss Reducing Measures

There are many simple and effective ways of improving the amount of heat that is retained within a house that are inexpensive to carry out. These measures should be used in tandem with changing the way in which a house is lived in during the winter, in order to reduce fuel consumption. The first consideration is to reduce the amount of draughts, in order to reduce the amount of heated air that escapes from the house. This, however, has to be balanced against the need for a house to be ventilated, so that airborne water vapour can be removed from the house, rather than allowing it to get into the fabric of the house, where it may lead to damp problems.

Roof Insulation

The greatest amount of energy is lost through the roof of a house as heat rises, so ensure that the thickness of roof insulation is sufficient, as this will reduce the amount of heat lost, in the same way that wearing a hat in winter keeps us warmer.

There are many different types of roof insulation currently available that can be used to reduce the amount of heat loss through the ceilings of rooms below attics. Each has different characteristics and not all are suited to the particular requirements that many of our older houses have to be able to 'breathe'.

Draught Proofing

As a considerable amount of heat is lost from the gaps around external doors and windows, by ensuring that draught-proofing tapes are applied around these features, this will reduce the level of draughts during the winter months. These draught strips can relatively easily be removed for redecoration or when they have lost their performance. Chimneys in rooms where the fires are not to be lit over the winter might be blocked up temporarily to restrict the amount of heated air being lost up a chimney during the winter. During the summer, however, chimneys can usefully circulate air around the house and allow any lingering dampness to evaporate before the next winter. A chimney should not normally be permanently sealed up without some ventilation being allowed, or dampness might accumulate within the unused stack. Just as a house should be prepared for winter, the same applies to the occupants, who are likely to wear more clothing, rather than relying on higher room temperatures as we move towards a more fuel-conscious future.

Curtains, Blinds and Net Curtains

Windows in most older houses were designed either to have shutters or curtains, and these should be closed during the winter when the sun goes down to ensure that the amount of heat loss is reduced. Thermal linings can be inserted into existing curtains to improve their level of thermal insulation.

The curtain on the right has been lined with thermal linings and the difference is noticeable during daylight by comparison with the other unlined curtain.

Thermal-insulation fabric can be fitted inside existing curtains to increase the amount of heat that is retained within a house.

Windows on south walls are potentially heat-gaining areas, while the sun is shining; windows on north walls are areas where heat is quickly lost if curtains are not closed – it may be worth considering keeping these shut in any unused north-facing rooms, even by day. Even with the main curtains open, a minimal improvement can be made by using net curtains, which allow light through but which create a slight obstacle to air movement acting directly on the glass.

Curtains can be used to cover doors as well as windows. There are devices that lift the closed curtain up when the door is opened. This ingenious device was developed by the Victorians, who were very familiar with the need to keep as much heat in a house as possible.

A door curtain lined with thick material does not take up a significant amount of space next to a door.

Blinds can be made with layers of fabric insulation in them to ensure that windows are protected from the cold air outside. The most important windows to concentrate on first are the windows on the north side of the house, where more heat is lost than in other parts of the house.

Net curtains may also help resist overheating in summer by reflecting sunlight.

Net curtains might improve the thermal insulation of a room slightly if they can create a layer of relatively still air between the glass and the curtain.

Where radiators are situated under windows, there is likely to be considerable heat loss if the heat can rise up behind the curtain and out through the glass, so fixing a shelf over the radiator to deflect warmed air to the room side of the curtains might be a sensible measure in situations like this, or perhaps introducing a thermally-lined blind behind the line of the existing window sill.

Shutters

Shutters are an important feature of some types of windows and the shutters should be closed at dusk, or perhaps if the room is not being used, to ensure that the maximum amount of heat is retained within the room.

Timber shutters are effective at keeping more heat in a room at night than curtains. If the shutters are covered with curtains as well, this will reduce the amount of heat lost through the window.

Secondary Glazing

Secondary glazing is a more expensive option than curtains, but this type of glazing can sometimes be designed to be applied over the inside of the windows during the winter and removed during the summer. The most important consideration, when fitting secondary glazing, is that the internal architectural features should not be cut or damaged in order to make the glazing fit. The glazing itself should be modified to fit around the architectural features of the house, to ensure that they are not damaged or lost, and so that future generations are not deprived of these elements. Our need to conserve heat may be a serious problem to us for the foreseeable future, but it may not be a problem for our descendants in the far future, so we should try not to destroy their history.

The most successful secondary glazing is usually only visible from the outside, where a double reflection is visible in the window. So care has to be taken to ensure that any internal subdivisions in the glazing match up with those on the window.

Windows like these benefit from secondary glazing in terms of reducing the amount of heat lost through the window and the only noticeable feature from the exterior is a double reflection in the glass.

Energy Reduction

Energy-saving light bulbs can be used within most types of existing light fittings, though there are deficiencies in the design and performance of the early versions; these problems promise to be ironed out in the near future.

Methods of Generating Energy for the Home

There are many ways of generating heat or electricity for use in the home. Making use of naturally available resources is most likely to be the popular way forward in the future. These encompass using solar panels of various types for heating water and for generating electricity, wind power for generating electricity and heat pumps, which gather low levels of ambient heat from the environment and concentrate it.

Timber is the oldest fuel for fires and, providing new trees are grown to replenish the equivalent amount of firewood and to keep absorbing the carbon dioxide released from the burning, then this, in theory, broadly balances out this method of heating in environmental terms.

The earliest form of heating was a wood fire, which was coupled with warm clothing to keep occupants of a room warm.

Solar panels have become more popular in the twenty-first century and there has to be care and consideration as to their location on an older house. There are planning restrictions regarding these in certain situations and on certain types of buildings. They should be located away from main elevations to avoid detracting from the overall appearance of the house. Often solar panels are sited on the rear roofs of a house, so that they are most visible from the garden. Sensitivity in the location of these panels, which nevertheless have to be positioned to face the sun, is the most important aspect of this type of installation. But, as is also the case with satellite dishes, there is often no reason to place solar collectors – particularly those used to generate electricity – on a house if there is adequate space in the garden.

Solar panels have to be located to face the sun, but care is necessary in where they are located on a house to minimize their impact, and not be out of balance with the architecture.

Where solar panels are located on the rear of a house, are less visible from the road, but may be seen from the rear garden, so care is necessary in considering the full implications of their locations, even when they have to be located to face the sun. Here they have been able to follow the line of the windows below.

Water Conservation

There are many ways in which the amount of water that is used in a house can be reduced by the occupants being careful with the amount of water they use. Once the amount of water used has been addressed, then consider making the most use of the existing rainwater that is collected around the house by downpipes.

A water butt was a traditional way of saving water to use on home grown fruit and vegetables.

Gardens

The Victorians prided themselves in the amount of fruit and vegetables that they could grow in their gardens. We now have freezers to store food, while our ancestors used storage jars to preserve their food for use in the winter.

Home-grown grapes reduce the amount of energy that is used up in transporting these from other countries when they are easy to grow, and global warming makes this likely to be easier for us.

A pear tree takes up little space and can produce significant quantities of pears that can be stored for use at other times of the year.

Fruit and vegetables preserved in jars use up less electricity than storing them in the freezer.

The Future

The future of older houses is to ensure that they remain as intact as possible for future generations to enjoy. Modifications or alterations should only be carried out where existing features can be retained and any new work is truly reversible, so that, if it were removed in the future, there would be no long-term loss to the house. Even the parts of a house that have been added recently are a part of the history of the house. The quality of materials that were used in the past may no longer be replicated to the same standard, so that any alterations in the future may be of a lesser quality than was previously available. In the future, the amount of energy available for producing new building materials may become more restricted than at present, which may mean that there will be a greater emphasis on building methods and materials that were used in the past.

Further Information

For more information about looking after old houses please visit the author's website, **www.oldhouse.info**

For more about the history and maintenance of old houses:

Claxton, Bevis, *Maintaining and Repairing Old Houses – A Guide to Conservation, Sustainability and Economy* (Crowood, 2008)

Collings, Janet, *Victorian and Edwardian Houses – A Guide to Care and Maintenance* (Crowood, 2008)

Index